28

The Military Genius of

ABRAHAM LINCOLN

ABRAHAM LINCOLN (1809–1865)
Sixteenth President of the United States

★ ★ ★ ★ ★ ★ ★ ★ ★ ★ ★ ★ ★

THE MILITARY GENIUS OF

Abraham Lincoln

AN ESSAY BY BRIGADIER-GENERAL COLIN R. BALLARD, C.B., C.M.G. ★ WITH A PREFACE BY FLETCHER PRATT ★ PHOTOGRAPHS FROM THE MESERVE COLLECTION

CLEVELAND AND NEW YORK

THE WORLD PUBLISHING COMPANY

Published by The World Publishing Company

Library of Congress Catalog Card Number: 52–5180

FIRST EDITION

PREFACE

IF ONE wishes to know something about one's own country, it is often a very good idea to ask a foreigner what he thinks of it. He may not be quite as well informed as a native, and he may not have all his details straight; but the details he does have enable him to form a judgment unaffected by local prejudices and local controversies. That is, by seeing things from a distance, he will have a better grasp of the whole picture.

In the present case, that grasp is practically the whole book; and it is not observable that General Ballard has missed any essential details. Also, in setting them out, he has produced what amounts to an extremely good short history of the war. It perhaps does not rest quite enough weight on the importance of the Western campaigns, but the primary purpose is to examine Lincoln's influence on strategy, and as Lincoln had a couple of pretty good strategists, named Grant and Sherman, out there, his influence was limited to keeping them on the job, and seeing they got what they needed.

General Ballard has also perhaps somewhat under-estimated the part factional politics played in Lincoln's selection of generals, and especially in his retention of McClellan in command, after that officer had demonstrated his incapacity for anything but leading a parade. But this is not really germane to the subject of the book. General Ballard proves convincingly that Lincoln chose good generals whenever there were good generals to choose, the striking case being the retention of Grant in the face of criticism. But the main concern here is with the higher strategy of the war as a whole, the sort of thing that was worked out during the late conflict by the heads of states meeting at various places around the world for conferences with peculiar names. Lincoln had

v

nobody to confer with; he had to do it alone, and in the course of examining how well he did it, General Ballard is required to demolish the legend that the President was a politician, whose bungling interference hampered the efforts of his generals and prolonged the war.

As a large part of this legend arises from the McClellan case, so a large part of the book deals with the period when McClellan was in command of the Army of the Potomac. The author has here gone to the original documents, including "McClellan's Own Story," and shows that few generals were ever less interfered with. Lincoln did not like McClellan's plan for the Peninsular campaign (in fact, it turned out to be a very bad one) but he acquiesced in it and gave the General everything he asked, except just one thing—the troops necessary for the defense of Washington.

It did not seem important to McClellan that these troops should be kept where they were and, in a pure military sense, as a matter of map maneuver, it perhaps was not. But war is not a map maneuver or a game of chess in which forces can be distributed to deal with the armed forces of the enemy to the best advantage. The political factors which support the war must be considered; indeed, Clausewitz has remarked that war is only an extension of political action. When this is forgotten, the art of war exists only in a vacuum. General Ballard shows that Lincoln never forgot it, and that he brought something new to war.

When Lincoln did make suggestions to his generals— and his "interference" was limited to presenting considerations for them to bear in mind—they were usually of the order of the two remarkable letters to Hooker during the Gettysburg campaign, and the non-military reader will perhaps be surprised to discover that they were nearly always right. The soldier is less so. In this book he is looking at the large features of war; the question of who grasped the over-all strategic situation,

who made the decisions through which the resources of
the North were developed and applied in such a fashion
as to be decisive. At the end of the path the author sees
Lincoln; and he lays his case strongly on the President's
first strategic decision, the proclamation of the blockade. In this, the book does a real service; we Americans
have generally confined ourselves to remarking that
there was such a thing as a blockade, describing how it
operated and what its effect was, without ever inquiring
on what grounds the project was originated.

There was no precedent whatever for such a blockade.
But it is precisely one of General Ballard's points that
there were no precedents for many of the things Lincoln
did, that he was a completely unconventional strategist.
There could be no precedents; as the book points out,
war had entered a new dimension, in which a new
echelon of command was imposed upon those already
existing—the over-all leader who develops the resources
of an entire nation. With that development there must
naturally go a need for strategic decisions in the topmost
echelon; what resources shall be developed, how they
shall be developed and applied.

I personally find it rather a pity that General Ballard
did not press matters further along this line, and draw
the obvious parallel with Jefferson Davis, who was also
a strategist, but one with conventional military training,
who thought in terms of Napoleonic maneuver. But
then, one could stand to have the book longer in many
respects, and it is perhaps one of its virtues that it
furnishes food for thought without attempting to tell
readers how to think.

General Ballard quotes significantly from Grant, with
regard to his first interview with the President: "All he
wanted or had ever wanted was someone who would
take the responsibility and act, and call on him for all
the assistance necessary, pledging himself to use all the
power of the government in rendering such assistance."

The very fact that such a statement was made demonstrates how often it had been necessary for Lincoln to enter the field of straight military strategy, as when he issued his war orders, and later, when Burnside felt he had to submit a plan of campaign and get it approved before going ahead.

But in that department also, in fulfilling the task he was so unwilling to assume, the author demonstrates that Lincoln was a decidedly greater Commander in Chief than he is generally given credit for being. He has (for instance) uncovered a dispatch neglected by most American writers, showing that Lincoln knew better than Grant what was needed when Early made his raid on Washington in 1864.

Such a book should have been written, such an estimate should have been made, after World War II showed that the kind of command Lincoln exercised had become a permanent feature of war. It is completely surprising to discover that it was written shortly after World War I; but that increases rather than destroys its validity today.

FLETCHER PRATT

February, 1952

CONTENTS

LIST OF SKETCH MAPS

ILLUSTRATIONS

LIST OF AUTHORS CONSULTED

Allan, William: *History of the Campaign of Gen. T. J. (Stonewall) Jackson in the Shenandoah Valley of Virginia from November 4, 1861, to June 17, 1862.* Philadelphia: 1880.

Charnwood, Lord (Godfrey Rathbone Benson): *Abraham Lincoln.* London: 1916.

Ford, Worthington Chauncey, editor: *A Cycle of Adams Letters, 1861–1865.* 2 vols., Boston: 1920.

Grant, Ulysses S.: *Personal Memoirs of U. S. Grant.* 2 vols. New York: 1885.

Henderson, G. F. R.: *Stonewall Jackson and the American Civil War.* 2 vols. London: 1898.

Johnson, Robert Underwood and Clarence Clough Buel, Editors: *Battles and Leaders of the Civil War.* 4 vols. New York: 1884–1888.

McClellan, George B.: *McClellan's Own Story.* New York: 1887.

Mahan, Alfred T.: *The Gulf and Inland Waters.* New York: 1885.

Maurice, Sir Frederick: *Robert E. Lee the Soldier.* London: 1925.

Military Historical Society of Massachusetts: *Papers, Vol. III. The Virginia Campaign of General Pope in 1862.* Boston: 1886.

Moore, Frank, Editor: *The Rebellion Record* (also issued as *Putnam's Record of the Rebellion*). 12 vols. New York: 1861–1868.

Paxson, Frederic L.: *The American Civil War.* New York: 1911.

Rhodes, James Ford: *History of the United States from the Compromise of 1850. Volumes III–VI.* New York: 1895–1906.

Ropes, John Codman: *The Story of the Civil War*. 2 vols. New York: 1894, 1898.

Sheridan, Philip H.: *Personal Memoirs of P. H. Sheridan*. 2 vols. New York: 1888.

Sherman, William T.: *Memoirs of General W. T. Sherman, Written by Himself*. 2 vols. New York: 1875, 1887.

Shotwell, Walter Gaston: *The Civil War in America*. 4 vols. London: 1923.

Swinton, William: *Campaigns of the Army of the Potomac*. 1866, 1882.

Wood, W. Birkbeck and J. E. Edmunds: *A History of the Civil War in the United States, 1861–5*. New York: 1905.

The Military Genius of

ABRAHAM LINCOLN

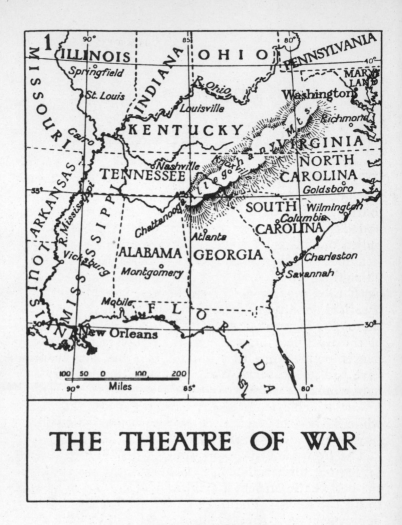

THE THEATRE OF WAR

SKETCH MAPS

Unionists = ████ and — — — — — —

Confederates = ▭ and ------------

Only those places are marked which are mentioned in the text

I

AN UNCONVENTIONAL STRATEGIST

THERE is a legend of the East which tells of three men—a carpenter, a tailor, and a holy man—who journeyed together. While they rested from the noonday heat beneath a spreading tree the carpenter pulled out his knife and cut down a branch which he fashioned roughly into the form of a woman; the tailor then unrolled his pack and stitched fragments of cloth into a garment for the figure; the holy man breathed upon it and it came to life. Each of the men thereupon claimed possession, declaring that his share of the work had been the most important; the carpenter pointed out that but for him the lady would have had no existence at all; the tailor urged that an ugly woman is worse than none, and that it was only his art which had made her existence worth having; while the holy man made the obvious remarks about the superiority of mind over matter.

The formation of an army may be roughly divided into three similar stages. The recruiting office plays the part of the carpenter and provides the raw material to fill the ranks. The tailor's part is taken by various departments who supply clothing, equipment, arms, and ammunition. The Commander and his General Staff infuse the life, which comprises discipline, training, morale, and strategy and tactics.

In bygone days sheer numbers very often decided a battle. As firearms improved they outweighed numbers; a small well-armed force can defeat a horde of savages. When opposing forces are anything like equal in numbers and armament the issue is decided by the moral factors—the discipline and valour of the troops, or the genius of the leader. There have been (and will be) cases where moral factors have triumphed over heavy physical odds.

In the American Civil War there is no doubt that Mr. Abraham Lincoln took a leading part as carpenter and tailor. To start with he had a mere handful of men; it was chiefly due to his energy that these were reinforced till there were more than a million well-armed men in the ranks. All historians agree in giving him credit.

But he did more than this—he took upon himself to control the broad lines of the strategy, and in some cases he even issued detailed orders for movements of troops. Here the chorus of praise changes to a note of denunciation. The military critics are especially severe, and long sermons have been written about the folly of amateur strategists, the wickedness of politicians who interfere with regular soldiers, the timidity, or to put it more bluntly the cowardice, which reigned in the offices at Washington and spread its baneful influence in the Federal Army of the North.

The following pages will show that in this case I do not agree with certain eminent critics. But this is treading on dangerous ground, and to avoid any possible ambiguity let me enunciate my theorem, after the fashion of Euclid, before attempting to prove it.

My belief is that Lincoln was solely responsible for the strategy of the North and proved himself a very capable strategist. But (a very big but) this does not mean that other politicians should try to follow his example. The general principles regarding amateur strategists and political interference in war have been proved by history—my point is that general principles do not govern a case of exceptional genius.

There is such a thing as damning with faint praise—but fulsome or exaggerated praise is even more fatal, so no attempt will be made to gloss over mistakes—which were not unfrequent. But most of these arose from unavoidable circumstances. Lincoln suddenly found himself called to supreme power at the head of a nation which was drifting into civil war. He had no knowledge of the theories of military science, no experience of operations in the field, no training in the technical side, no acquaintance with the theatre of war except such as could be derived from maps. Worse still, he had never met any of the men who were to lead his troops, and none of them had any experience of handling large forces. It is not too much to say that no commander ever started with a heavier handicap.

To soldiers of the old school there is something repugnant in the idea of an army being controlled from the desk of an office. I am an old soldier—*moi qui vous parle*—and know the strength of those old traditions. In childhood we were brought up on tales of the Black Prince at Crécy, of Henry V and the happy few who fought with him at Agincourt. Those were the days of shining armour, when a commander was above all things a *leader* and charged at the head of his knights.

Then came the first great evolution of warfare—in the form of drill : troops were drilled into a machine which could be manœuvred at the will of one man, who was the *tactician* : he must be well up with his leading ranks to note the lie of the ground and the dispositions of the foe, to seize the opportune moment. Those were the days of professional armies, small but well drilled, of gold lace and cocked hats : the days of great tacticians : Marlborough, who ' rides on the whirlwind and controls the storm ' : [1] Frederick the Great with his oblique attack : Napoleon, whose mere presence on the field was worth 40,000 men in the opinion of his great rival Wellington.

After the Napoleonic era armies increased in numbers

[1] Addison, *The Campaign.*

and the field of battle widened ; the commander could no longer exercise personal control, and it became clear that he must take up a post from which he could keep in touch with troops out of sight and spread over many miles of country. Those were the days of the military *strategist*, and we think at once of Von Moltke in his two great campaigns of 1866 and 1870. His forces were organized and his plans prepared before ever the clash of arms was heard—and his place was well in the rear of the fighting line. It is true that he was present at the battles of Sadowa and Gravelotte, but that was because his work as a strategist was over for the moment ; he had brought the troops on to the field, but left the handling of men to subordinates.

In the present century we have seen further evolution in warfare : no longer is the struggle confined to professional forces—whole nations were dragged into it, and those in the front line were supported by the industry and will power of those behind. The commander in the field was dependent on the statesman who organized the resources of the nation. The higher strategy and the distribution of the British troops, from Calais to Baghdad, was controlled from an office in London—and it is time to recognize that in a war of the nations this must be so.

For students of Military History, the chief interest of the American Civil War lies in the fact that in some respects it was the forerunner of modern conditions. A great nation, having only a small handful of professional soldiers, had to organize itself for a mighty struggle : operations were spread over hundreds of miles of country : natural resources, finance, industry, commerce, and politics were all big factors which had their weight in dictating the higher strategy.

This is why I call Lincoln the Strategist of the North—he was the forerunner of that which we now call the Higher Command.

The critics admit that it was necessary to have one man in control of the operations, and that Washington was the best place from which such control could be exercised. The fault they find is that Lincoln, being a civilian, interfered with professional soldiers, and thus did grievous harm to the cause of the North. Before this criticism can be answered we must look into the facts.

To revert for a moment to our legend of the East—it has various endings according to the moral which the storyteller wishes to deduce. In one version the lady went in chase of a gaudy butterfly and disappeared for ever in the jungle. The three friends, who had almost come to blows in the heat of passion, thereupon cooled down and resumed their arguments in a spirit of philosophic calm. Of course the moral is that personal interest obscures our powers of judgement.

Much of the history of the Civil War was written while passions were still smouldering, by men who had taken an active part in the mighty struggle. Such records have a very real value of their own, and there are few more interesting pictures of war than those found in *Battles and Leaders*; [1] they give us the human side of the battle-field, the atmosphere of the bivouac, the gossip of the camp fire. The authors speak with the authority of eye-witnesses; they were perfectly honest in their convictions and meant to be impartial in their opinions. But their convictions were deep, they had offered their lives in defence of them; their passions were roused by the stirring scenes they had gone through; affection and admiration for their leaders and brothers in arms introduce a personal factor; such feelings cannot be discarded by a proclamation of peace. Besides this, a soldier in a battle sees only a small section of the field, and the more that spot absorbs his gaze the

[1] *Battles and Leaders of the Civil War*. A collection of personal accounts by prominent generals on both sides.

more does it throw out of focus his view of the general operations. Strategy demands a wider and more detached judgement.

In England the most popular book on the war is Colonel Henderson's *Stonewall Jackson*. It might be thought that a British officer, far removed from American politics and from any personal association with either the Northern or the Southern armies, would be an impartial judge ; he certainly had no axe of his own to grind. But in his careful preparation of the book he visited the battle-fields of Virginia and got into touch with those who could give him intimate details about Jackson ; these persons, relatives and brother officers, had a passionate reverence for their hero, and Henderson's enthusiastic nature caught the infection to such an extent that he over-stated his case; a study of his book shows that he not only failed to appreciate the Northern leaders (and especially Lincoln), but by deriding Jackson's opponents he is unjust to Jackson himself. If we accept the idea that Lincoln was an interfering politician, that McClellan was cautious and unenterprising to the verge of timidity, and that during the first years the Northern leaders were ' mere pigmies ', it follows that it did not require a giant to overcome them.

My theory is that Lincoln had a fine grasp of the big situation. He realized that numbers, resources, and command of the sea were on his side ; these factors must eventually wear down the resistance of the South, provided that no opportunity were given to a clever enemy to deal a knock-out blow before the resources of the North were fully developed. Though he had no personal knowledge of the Southern leaders, his keen insight soon recognized their daring brilliance. At the same time he had his finger on the pulse of his own Federal States ; twenty-two of these declared for the Union, but they were not united in support of Lincoln.

There were men who honestly disagreed with his policy; there were politicians who had long haunted the corridors of White House and were disgruntled at seeing an unknown lawyer from the backwoods jumping in over their heads ; there were soldiers who had plans that would end the war in a month.

Lincoln was not the man to say ' L'Etat c'est moi ' ; but he might have said so without exaggeration. He had to keep his eye on his friends as well as on his enemies. A sudden blow at Washington, a dashing invasion of Maryland, Pennsylvania, or New York, an overwhelming defeat of the main field army, would raise an outburst from all discontented elements and might prove decisive. Attempts like these were always in the mind of Lee and Jackson, and there were moments when they were nearly carried through. Lincoln was aware of this, and therefore his first object was to avoid such blows until he was ready with his counter-stroke. It was not timidity or want of enterprise that kept so much of his force on the defensive, it was the wisdom of a strategist who could look ahead, it was the courage which faces censure and overrides the maxims of conventional warfare.

Granted that there were occasions when this caution was overdone, and when bolder action might have shortened the war. The policy of caution, however wise in the circumstances, was too obvious. Lee and Jackson seized upon it as a vulnerable point and made the most of it ; but it was founded upon a rock against which their skill and valour dashed themselves in vain, and in the long last it was justified by the result.

If this premise can be proved it accounts for many incidents which have been severely criticized ; it also raises Lee and Jackson to a higher level than that of men who have to fight against timorous and incapable amateurs. Their strategy was equally fine—they realized that the physical factors, numbers and re-

sources, were against them; they therefore concentrated their efforts on bringing into play the moral
factors—' mystify and mislead your enemy ', ' attack
is the best form of defence ', ' surprise is the greatest
weapon in war '.

We have then the two opponents, Lincoln and Lee,
foemen worthy of each other's steel. Each had his own
form of strategy perfectly adapted to his own situation; Lee striving to get in a blow before the net
enclosed him, Lincoln avoiding the blow until his net
was ready to be cast.

Lee had the more attractive part to play; the
boldness of his strokes are the delight of military
critics; ' l'audace, l'audace, et toujours l'audace '
appeals to even the most unscientific soldier; a struggle
against superior numbers enlists the sympathy of
everybody.

But the brilliance of Lee's exploits should not be
allowed to dazzle our eyes to such an extent that
we miss the significance of Lincoln's strategy. This
strategy was not on the conventional lines of Napoleon
and Von Moltke, but it is just in its originality that its
beauty comes out. As Henderson says, ' military
genius shows itself first in character, and, second, in the
application of the grand principles of war.' The
application of grand principles—not the mere knowledge
of them. There is no difficulty in learning by heart the
Ten Commandments, the trouble begins when they
have to be applied. Like the poet, the strategist is
born, not made, and Lincoln had the character of a
born strategist. He could not apply the grand principles because he had never had an opportunity to
study them; but instinctively he grasped the main
facts and gave them their proper value. It is undeniable that a knowledge of the technical side of war
would have been of use to him; it would have helped
him to pick up the threads more quickly and surely;

it would have enabled him to detect the weak points in his own forces. But theoretical knowledge is like a powerful drug, of great worth in the hands of a wise man but a deadly poison when misapplied.

Napoleon's methods were admirably fitted to his own times and his circumstances, and were so successful that they have been hailed as eternal principles, applicable to all times and all circumstances ; the conventional theorist still clings to them ; Lincoln would have discarded some and applied others in the right place.

The Athenian soldier (or was it the Spartan ?) drew his sword and threw away the scabbard as a sign that he meant business. The subaltern in the Great European War went a step farther and threw away not only his scabbard but his sword as well—it hampered him while climbing over barbed wire or wading through mud more than knee-deep. The sword, a quaint relic of medieval warfare, is the outward sign of certain doctrines which still cramp the movements of those who burden themselves with them.

' The mules of Frederick the Great went through twenty campaigns but still remained mules.' There have been other mules since the days of Frederick, but Abraham Lincoln was not one of them.

II

THE GREAT ILLUSION

THE only excuse for this chapter is that it was once used as a lecture to British officers whose knowledge of American History was limited ; we knew that Columbus discovered the New World and that George Washington had an axe ; he cut down a cherry tree and severed connexion with the Mother Country ; after that there were incidents painful to British observers, but, like Nelson, we know when to apply the telescope to our blind eye, so there comes a hiatus in the history of America. Interest is awakened once again by the Civil War.

There are plenty of histories to fill up the gap, but for the military student, who is more concerned with strategy than political development, the following notes may serve as an overture to the war.

Superior persons, who know by heart the list of American presidents as English schoolboys know their list of kings and queens, may be advised to skip to the next chapter.

The Constitution. In the last half of the seventeenth century the adventurers of the New World were taking root as colonists. In the first half of the succeeding century we find the Atlantic coast dotted with prosperous settlements of Anglo-Saxon blood (except Rip Van Winkle), while the French had pushed southwards from Canada and struck the Mississippi. Sturdy pioneers, hunters, and trappers were spreading inland over the Alleghanies and were driving the Red Indians westwards.

During the first half of the eighteenth century the

young colonies acquired a good deal of independence regarding their own affairs, but were still linked to the Mother Country by the fear of foreign aggression. Though the navies of Spain and Holland were no longer a menace there still remained France, whose mighty monarch, Louis XIV, saw the value of the New Continent. After Wolfe took Quebec in 1759 the Treaty of Paris (1763) gave Canada to England, the French retaining only the territory west of the Mississippi. The colonies no longer needed the protection of the Royal Navy, and at the same time the development of their industries made them self-supporting. So it came that the spirit of independence grew strong. The British Government still claimed the right to impose taxation, which was justified by their expenditure on naval and military forces. The Americans insisted on the principle of ' No taxation without representation '.

Successive Governments at Westminster imposed a Stamp Act (1765), repealed it, imposed other taxes, bungled them, revoked the charter of Massachusetts, and closed the port of Boston. These vagaries, which arose partly from a desire to discredit their predecessors, aroused the temper of the colonists and caused some local rioting. When the more serious citizens were drawn into the question the discontent took serious form in the Declaration of Independence (1776). After five years of struggle the decisive event occurred at Yorktown where Cornwallis, cut off from reinforcements by a French fleet, was forced to surrender. It had been evident for some time that England could not hold by force so great a territory inhabited by bold and determined men. Another change of Government simplified matters, and the preliminaries of peace were discussed. In 1783 the peace was signed which heralded the birth of a new nation. But the rebellion was against King George III and his Ministers; it was not a social revolution. The rebels were neither anarchists, nor communists, nor sans-culottes, nor Bolsheviks. Credit may be given to the Anglo-Saxon character for the fact that there was no vicious struggle for power, no upset of the decencies of normal existence. Life went on as before, and it only remained to install a new form of Government in the place of the departed. This was not an easy task; the country was a thousand miles in extent from north to south, and from east to west it was practically more, owing to the badness of the communications; there were various interests to be reconciled; but there were wise men who applied themselves to the task, and their solution was the Constitution of 1789, which holds good to the present day.

There were to be thirteen States. Each was to be independent regarding internal affairs; its Governor was to be elected locally; it was to have its own Legislature and complete power over its militia and its revenues. But for certain common interests they were to form a partnership under a Federal Government which sat at Washington.

The population, however, was spreading westwards and new tracts of country were being opened out. These places were officially styled Territories and were administered by the Federal Government. When a Territory could claim 60,000 inhabitants it applied for formal recognition as a State and was granted home rule on the same terms as the others. By 1850 twenty-two new States had been added to the original thirteen, and Kansas and Nebraska were applying for recognition.

The Federal Government has power over foreign relations, peace and war, the navy and the standing army. In order to provide revenue it imposes and collects import taxes. The forts, arsenals, dockyards, and custom-houses throughout the country are the property of the Federal Government.

The Legislature consists of a Senate and a House of Representatives, who together form Congress. Each State elects two senators and a number of representatives proportionate to its population.

The Federal Executive is very much centralized in the President, who selects his own Ministers, appoints Ambassadors, and has a very large amount of patronage in selecting officers of the Union. He is chosen by a somewhat complicated process which is intended to base the election on the popular vote of the whole country.

Once elected the President holds the reins for four years ; he can only be removed by impeachment ; as he nominates and dismisses Ministers at his own will his power is almost unlimited. The official check upon him is that Congress, by a majority of two-thirds, can disavow his action. An unofficial but more effective check is the prospect of the day of reckoning at the next election. He has no control over finance or the Legislature.

It is a matter of opinion whether a disguised autocracy is the best form of government in time of peace ; history shows that in time of war it has many advantages ; Alexander the Great, Frederick the Great, Napoleon the Great were heads of their States as well as leaders of their armies. On the other hand there are few cases of councils which have conducted war with success ; Allied Councils, however firm and loyal the alliance, do not arrive at those quick and clear-cut decisions which are so necessary in crises ; the seven great Coalitions against Napoleon are records of mistimed co-operation and wasted effort ; the Aulic Councils are a byword of incapacity.

This does not imply that the autocrat need do all the work himself ; he may appoint deputies to any extent to take charge of various departments and to command the armies ; these in turn may delegate authority—

till the subaltern in charge of a picket or the corporal in command of a party of scouts finds himself independent for the moment. But the chain of authority and responsibility must be vertical, not horizontal. When the responsibility for decision and action is shared, history shows that the results are bad.

A good example of delegated authority is that provided by Von Bismarck and Von Moltke. As Chancellor, Von Bismarck had the supreme power, but in Von Moltke he had a general of recognized standing on whom he could rely implicitly. He therefore handed over to Von Moltke the whole responsibility for the army and the strategy, and confined himself to providing money and giving orders for the commencement of operations. Von Moltke in his turn appointed Von Roon to do the work of carpenter and tailor, reserving to himself questions of training and strategy. This division of labour worked with perfect smoothness and was a big factor in the success of the Prussians. The strategy is therefore Von Moltke's, and he gets the credit for it.

Lincoln had no Von Moltke; there were men to whom he could apply for technical advice, but he did not feel complete confidence in any of them; he left to them certain details but he retained considerable powers in his own hands.

It is important to remember this. Many people think that he was merely a civilian organizer, sitting in an office in Washington, who occasionally interfered either from petulance or panic with his generals. Plans may be drawn up by subordinates, to whom credit can be given for the foresight and imagination they display; but the responsibility lies with the Chief who accepts or rejects or amends the plan. This responsibility lay entirely with Lincoln; he struck the key-note; and this establishes him as the Strategist of the North. He must take the credit or bear the blame.

Slavery. In the eighteenth century slavery was recognized in civilized countries ; the opening up of a new country demands a large amount of manual labour, so slavery was flourishing in America, especially in the South, when the Constitution of 1789 came into force.

Some slave-traders treated their human chattels with brutality, and there were pitiable scenes in the slave-market of New Orleans ; families were broken up and girls were sold into something worse than bondage.

The Abolitionists, who held that slavery is contrary to humanity, seized on the worst incidents to prove their case, and preached a crusade.

The extremists, on the other side, quoted the Old Testament as recognizing slavery, and added that, even if emancipation were theoretically advisable, in practice it would mean the ruin of the slaves : the negroes were of a low order of intelligence and could no more take care of themselves than children in the nursery : they were constitutionally lazy and would starve if not compelled to work : they had no self-restraint, and liberty would soon degenerate into licence : emancipation in San Domingo had been followed by hideous massacres : there were certainly some abuses which could be redressed, but on the whole the slave was no worse off than the ' mean white ' in the slums of New York and Chicago : the Abolitionists should begin with the beam in their own eye.

Such doctrines naturally received the support of the slave-owners, who, apart from all ethics, saw that abolition would deprive them of the labour so necessary on cotton and tobacco plantations.

The Abolitionists retorted that a starving freeman must be happier than a well-fed slave, and if any slaves were contented, they had no right to be so. Among the Northerners, who had no personal interest in slavery, their propaganda found a sympathetic audience. Moderate men on both sides were prepared to com-

promise on the subject. They agreed that slavery as
an institution was contrary to humanity and civilization, but sooner than upset the economic situation by a
sudden and wide measure of emancipation they were
prepared to restrict any further extension of it, abolish
the abuses of the slave-markets, and let emancipation
come gradually as the negroes became fit for it. Slavery
had disappeared in the Northern States without any
violent legislation ; it was on the decrease in the centre.
Professor Paxson says : ' It is reasonably clear to-day
that the South would of herself have discarded slavery
in another generation ; that the New Nationalism
would have come about without the Civil War.'

The Abolitionists, however, would hear of no compromise with the evil thing—no gradual movement—
no compensation for the owners ; nothing but a clean
and immediate sweep would satisfy them.

The dispute was advanced a stage in 1854. Henry
Clay, an ardent moderate, had devised and carried a
measure known as the ' Missouri Compromise ' ; this
established the principle that slavery was illegal north
of a certain geographical line (known as Mason and
Dixon's line). The Territories of Kansas and Nebraska
were applying for recognition as States. According
to the Missouri Compromise, as they lay to the north
of the line they must be ' Free ' States. According to
the original Constitution they would have the right to
settle for themselves, after recognition, whether they
would permit slavery. The Democrats had sufficient
votes to pass the Kansas-Nebraska law, which repealed
the Missouri Compromise.

This shifted the issue from the question of slavery to
a point of Constitutional Law. The Southerners
maintained the theory of Calhoun, that they were
independent States and that interference by the
Federal Government with their internal affairs was
a breach of the Constitution : if the Constitution

were violated each State would have the right to secede.

The Northern leaders saw that if this principle were accepted it would lead to a sort of political blackmail ; any State which had a grievance would threaten to secede, and the partnership would be broken up. Webster made a ringing appeal—' Liberty *and* Union, now and forever, one and inseparable.'

Needless to say neither side convinced the other. The Abolitionists made no secret of their intention of forcing their views if they obtained political power, so the Southerners forestalled them by taking action.

Four days after the election of Abraham Lincoln, South Carolina called a convention to face the crisis. Though Lincoln himself was a moderate, the Southerners believed that the Abolitionists would force his hand, so they proclaimed Secession. Six other States joined them and formed the Confederacy ; they elected Mr. Jefferson Davis as their President and established a Government which sat first at Montgomery in Alabama, and was moved in June 1861 to Richmond in Virginia.

To recapitulate the causes of the war : the existence of slavery was an anomaly in a civilized country and was the first issue ; the Kansas-Nebraska question brought it forward from the realm of ethics into the political arena ; the issue then shifted to the Right of Secession, and on this question the war was fought.

That this second issue was the main one is proved by many speeches on both sides, and by the fact that moderate Abolitionists fought in the ranks of the South, while among the Unionists were many who had no strong opinions about emancipation, and some who went so far as to believe that slavery was the best condition for the negro. It is, however, equally clear that the second issue would never have arisen unless the first one had raised it.

In England sympathy was divided and there were

changes of opinion. Two groups had definite views : those engaged in the cotton industry found their supply of raw material cut off by the blockade of the Southern ports—and wanted the war to stop : the adventurers, who were making fortunes by slipping through the blockade, wanted it to go on for ever. Disinterested persons at first based their views on *Uncle Tom's Cabin*, over which our great-grandmothers shed tears ; it was the best seller of its day, and still holds a place on our bookshelves by the side of *Uncle Remus* and *Huckleberry Finn*. But the newspapers explained that hunting negroes with bloodhounds was not the normal occupation of American gentlemen, so the pendulum swung the other way.

In 1863 opinion again reverted to its first impression, and the change came when the North was beginning to show its power. The American author, Owen Wister, says : 'The London *Times* and *Saturday Review* had lately been quoting the Bible as sanction for slavery ; for England dearly loves the Bible ; but now many voices in London became sure that slavery was wicked ; for England dearly loves success.' He might, however, have added that issues which even in America were not too clear would scarcely be better understood elsewhere. In English dictionaries ' Federal ' and ' Confederate ' are synonymous terms, while to stout monarchists there is little difference between Republican and Democrat. So why should Federal Republicans fight against Confederate Democrats ? When it appeared that there were Democrats fighting for the Federals and Republicans fighting for the Confederates, the permutations became too much for us—so we drew a line on our map between North and South and left it at that.

Colonel Henderson, writing thirty years later, voices the modern view :

' I am very strongly of opinion that any fair-minded man can feel equal sympathy with both Federals and Confederates.

Both were so absolutely convinced that their cause was just that it is impossible to conceive either Northerner or Southerner acting otherwise than he did. If Stonewall Jackson had been a New Englander, educated in the belief that secession was rebellion, he would assuredly have shed the last drop of his blood in defence of the Union ; if Ulysses Grant had been a Virginian, imbibing the doctrine of States' rights with his mother's milk, it is just as certain that he would have worn the Confederate grey.'

A professor of American History, pursuing the subject, has pointed out that in a quarrel both sides cannot be right. True. But both sides can be wrong.

It was the violence of the extremists—Abolitionists who shrieked about cruelty and Secessionists who shrieked about tyranny and intolerance—which stirred up bitterness and broke the bonds of kinship.

The moderates must take their share of the blame. They were in a big majority, and if they had met on neutral ground they could have resisted the pressure of the wings. Instead of this they allowed the political parties to cut a line which soon became an open gulf between them. It would be too much to expect from political foresight to say that any statesman ought to have foreseen the end—the loss of 600,000 young lives and the expenditure of hundreds of millions of dollars (enough to have compensated all the slave-owners). But the big men, and there were big men on both sides, might have seen farther than they did. ' Those behind cried : Forward ! While those in front cried : Back ! ' The minority behind shouted loudest, and the majority in front allowed themselves to be pushed into the gulf.

Nor was the general public free from blame. It extends a humorous indulgence to its politicians and allows a discount for platform effect. Certain States had threatened secession on former occasions, but nothing came of it—it was all bluff. The Abolitionists had used all sorts of threats against slavery and secession, but they would never enforce them by arms ; it was all bluff.

This is a thoroughly Anglo-Saxon frame of mind. We are not a race of swashbucklers ; we look upon war as hideous and wasteful ; we are too self-satisfied to be jealous of other nations ; at the same time we are not afraid of them. So we tell ourselves that war is the Great Illusion. Our Ministers declare that 'relations with Foreign Powers are friendly'; any increased expenditure on army or navy would be 'provocative'; even a statesman who foresees danger would feel indecent in uttering a warning aloud ; journalists who are less restrained are dubbed scaremongers. We have no use for Cassandra and are not going to be frightened by the first cry of 'Wolf!'

But if not an aggressive race we are a fighting one ; the Anglo-Saxon does not make war readily but he makes it long. The traditional gambit is to open with a contemptible little army and then, after the first reverse, expand it to about twenty times its original size. So history shows the army of Sir John Moore driven out of the Spanish Peninsula in 1809 and the French driven out five years later : General Gordon overpowered at Khartoum in 1885 and avenged by Kitchener in 1898 : the Boer War beginning with disasters in 1899 and dragged out till 1902 : the Great War opening with the retreat from Mons and fought out through more than four years. Of course each war is the absolute last—a war to end wars ; the wolf is dead and his race is extinct ; so once more war is put back on the shelf and is labelled the Great Illusion.

In America both sides were Anglo-Saxons, so the Great Illusion was raised to the power of two. Had the Mexicans collected an army to avenge their defeat of 1847 the Federal Government would have done something about it. Had an unknown tribe of Indians, twenty thousand strong, made an unexpected appearance in the west they would have been taken seriously.

But the Southerners were not Mexicans and the Northerners were not Redskins, and nobody had put on the war-paint.

Therefore the public comforted itself with the reflection that neither side had any army with which to make war, so the politicians, who had a common meeting ground at Washington, would take care to avoid it.

But that is just where the public went wrong and had to pay for its mistake—it is politicians who make war; soldiers make peace.

III

FROM LOG CABIN TO WHITE HOUSE

THIS book is not a study of Lincoln's career and character : it is merely an attempt to put the proper value on his military work. But it is necessary to glance, very briefly, at his life before he became President, just to see how his education and surroundings fitted him, or rather unfitted him, for the control of an army.

Early Days. Lincoln's grandfather was one of those who crossed the mountains in 1780 and settled with his family in Kentucky ; there he was killed by Indians four years later.

Thomas, youngest of his three sons, was a typical pioneer and hunter, constantly shifting his home farther westwards. His first wife, Nancy, was the daughter of a Virginian landowner. Their first child was Sarah, who grew up to become Mrs. Grigsby.

The second child, Abraham, was born on 12th February 1809. He was only eight years old when his mother died. A year or two later Thomas married again ; his second wife was the widow of a Mr. Johnston, and she brought with her to the new home a son John Johnston. She devoted herself to Sarah and Abraham, and entirely won their affection.

As Thomas Lincoln was always breaking new soil, young Abraham grew up in the school of the woods with Dame Nature as his earliest teacher—not the soft and gentle nature of the poets, but a stern old mother of the Spartan type. Of regular education he had very little ; occasionally a wandering schoolmaster came by for a month or two, and yet all the school days added together would scarcely have made one year. But the stepmother encouraged him, and the boy had a liking for his books. We used to be shown a picture of good little Abe doing sums on a spade with a lump of chalk by the light of a log fire. A moral picture. But the cabin was something like Robinson Crusoe's cave and, if memory serves me right, had a bear's skin and a tomahawk in it—such details spoilt the moral, for no fellow can be unhappy when he wears leather pants like a Red Indian and does not have to go to school.

Nor can I find much else of edification in the early days of my hero. An honest, healthy-minded lad, certainly, with a very tender heart ; but able to use his fists and play practical jokes, much like others of his age. All through his life he took incorrigible delight in telling ' a little story ' which was often broad in its humour—sadly disconcerting to the biographers who want to make a Sunday school story out of him. We can pass over those first twenty years.

1829–54. And indeed the records of the next twenty-five years are little more than chronicles of small beer unless we look below the surface. Not that he was idle—he was busy with many things. Not that he lacked ambition—far from it—but it was the clean ambition which will only spend its full energy on a cause which is worthy of it. He seems always to be waiting. Something like a knight-errant who waits for a damsel to be rescued or a dragon to be slain. Tilting sometimes at a windmill, like the melancholy knight, then chatting in a wayside inn with Sancho Panza and the passers-by. He neither smoked nor drank, but talked enough to make up for these deficiencies.

To all appearances these were lean years. But there are those who believe that they were not without fruit. Lincoln was studying that very complex thing which may be called the soul of the American nation, learning to love it and serve it, fitting himself for the time when he should come to control it.

Two voyages down the Mississippi in cargo-boats widened the horizon of the youth from the backwoods, and gave him glimpses of city life. Then assistant store-keeper in the small village of New Salem; store ' petered out '. An expedition against Indians in North Illinois; also petered out. Part owner of another store; the senior partner died of drink and left Lincoln heir to the bankruptcy—it is satisfactory to note that he paid up everything in course of time.

Did odd jobs for farmers, and did them well : be-came assistant land surveyor : was considered to have risen in life when appointed local postman. He hardly ever had a couple of dollars in his pocket, and hardly ever felt the need of them.

In the final choice of a career he hesitated whether to become a lawyer or a blacksmith; it is said that the forge seemed to offer better pecuniary results. But though a strong man, delighting in the strength of his arms, he was still more conscious of mental power, and sought to use it. Unmethodical in the small affairs of daily life, he was intensely logical in his thoughts; he established his major premise and reduced it to the simplest possible form of words, then drove home his point by the analogy of a ' little story '. To such a mind the law has irresistible attraction. In '37 he was taken into partnership by an old friend and settled down to business as a lawyer in Springfield. The business was successful enough to pay his modest bills and to earn him considerable respect in the local circle.

In '33 began the one romance of his life; he fell in love with Miss Ann Rutledge, but they had scarcely become engaged when she fell ill and died. This tragedy threw him into a phase of despondency which came near to unhinging his mind ; it may have been the cause of the melancholy moods which haunted him from time to time.

A year or two later he again became engaged to a Miss Mary Owens ; the affair seems to have been arranged by the lady's sister ; there was no enthusiastic devotion on either side and no tragedy in its termination.

In '39 Miss Mary Todd came from Kentucky to stay with a sister in Springfield. Lincoln proposed to her, but went through three years of hesitation and heart-searching before he married her in November '42. Though there was never a hint of scandal about their married life, there has been controversy about their happiness. Evidence shows that Abraham was guilty of shabby hats, muddy boots, and ' little stories '.

Politics. When only twenty-three years of age the future President began to dabble in local politics ; after one or two failures he was elected to the State Legislature in '34, and kept his seat for eight years. The politics were very local ; the young State was chiefly interested in developing its roads, canals, and later on its railways. In such matters the legislators were more enthusiastic than wise, judging from the fact that for some years the State had to suspend payment of interest on its bonds. Young Lincoln did not create any striking impression, nor did he adopt any very definite ' platform ' ; this may seem strange in a man who could think so clearly—but he was still waiting. And yet he enjoyed the game of politics for the game's sake, and picked up some experience in the ways of politicians. He gained sufficient influence to aim at Congress, and after some rebuffs he was elected. For two years he represented Illinois at Washington, but in '49 he lost his seat and returned to his office in Springfield. To close this period of his career let me

quote a few words from Lord Charnwood—sad that
space does not permit me to quote all of him :

'It is hard to resist the impression that Lincoln was at this
time a tired man, disappointed as to the progress of his career
and probably also disappointed and somewhat despondent about
the possibilities of good service that lay open to politicians.'

1854. From his earliest days Lincoln hated slavery
as an accursed thing. 'If slavery is not wrong nothing
is wrong.' On one of his trips to New Orleans he had
visited the slave-market, and the memory of it dwelt
with him. Yet he disagreed with the methods and
violence of the Abolitionists. There was in him a touch
of the Divine Nature which loves not sin but loves the
sinner, and he would not accept some instances of
cruelty as a proof of the iniquity of all slave-owners.
Besides this he stood firmly for the original Constitution
of ' the fathers ', under which slavery was not illegal :
any direct attack on it would cause an outburst which
might threaten the Union. Nevertheless he believed
that emancipation would come when the nation and the
slaves were fit for it—' in God's good time '. And so,
though he had all the energy and enthusiasm of a
reformer, he restrained himself with patience till he
could see a real and practical solution of the problem.

In '54 the Kansas-Nebraska law, which has already
been mentioned, passed through Congress ; it foreshadowed an extension of slavery in the Territories.
For Lincoln this was a call to arms. He had been in
doubt as to the best means of suppressing the slavery
that already existed ; he was in no doubt at all that
it was necessary to prevent any extension of it.

It was the Democrats who had passed the Kansas-
Nebraska law ; they had succeeded in doing so because
they were united, with a clear policy, while the opposition, though numerically strong, was disorganized and
weak. The old Whig party was in a state of decay ;
its great leaders, Webster and Clay, had died in '52 ;

its policy on slavery had always been vague, and now that slavery had become the first question the party ceased to exist. Its place was taken by the Republicans, whose platform was solid and square—no extension of slavery.

Lincoln had called himself a Whig, but had shown himself a bit of a free-lance now and then. He now found that he could enrol himself in the ranks of the Republicans, and prepared himself for battle. Chance threw in his path a formidable opponent, with whom he fought a long duel which gained him recognition as a champion.

This opponent was the famous Stephen Douglas. He had been Senator for Illinois since '47, and was now a leader of the Democrats and responsible for the Kansas-Nebraska law. From time to time he came back to his State to take part in the local elections.

Lincoln had tried to become a candidate in '56, but at the last moment withdrew in order to avoid splitting votes. This was a real sacrifice, and he was ambitious enough and human enough to feel personal disappointment. In '58 Douglas appeared again to seek his own re-election, and this time Lincoln was the official candidate of the Republicans.

Douglas was a very formidable rival. A small, fiery man, full of vitality, with much experience, he was regarded as an expert in the political field. Confident in himself, he agreed to follow the usual custom and meet Lincoln in debate in front of mass meetings. The public came in crowds to hear them, and it was generally expected that ' the Little Giant would wipe the floor with Abe '. Lincoln failed to win the election, but his clear and simple arguments stuck in the minds of his audience ; his words were easily remembered and were often quoted ; he was a man of mark, not only in Illinois, but throughout the States. A couple of years later the duel was renewed, this time on a wider field.

Before the election of a President it is the custom in America for each party to hold a 'convention' of its own supporters for the purpose of choosing a candidate. The system is fair enough, but sometimes reveals differences of opinion within the party which put a severe strain on party allegiance. In '60 the Republicans held their convention at Chicago; several names were put forward, including those of Seward, Chase, and Lincoln. After a vigorous contest Lincoln 'received the ticket'. This was a surprise to most of the Republicans themselves, but, in spite of some heart-burning, they all gave him loyal support.

Amongst the Democrats, on the other hand, there was a split. Douglas had taken as his catchword 'the everlasting principle of popular sovereignty'. Lincoln seized on these words and underlined them, but added that whereas Douglas intended them to mean that the people had a right to extend slavery, they must also mean that the people had a right to suppress it. This interpretation was disconcerting to the Democrats. When they held their convention Douglas stuck to his words with much courage. But there were some who regarded popular sovereignty as liberty only so long as they themselves were the sovereigns; they were wise enough to see that a day might come when the power would pass into other hands and popular sovereignty would be tyranny. Douglas got a majority and was the official candidate, but the minority repudiated him and put up a candidate of their own. This split among the Democrats paved the way to success for Lincoln, who had the Republicans united behind him.

On the 6th November 1860 he was elected President, but his term of office did not begin till 4th March.

The whole object of the above notes is simply to bring out two facts. First, the statesman who was called to the head of a nation in the hour of crisis had

no experience of administration or of the executive side
of government. Second, the Strategist who was
forced to assume control of armed forces had no
knowledge of military affairs. In the fifty years of
his life he had formed a wide circle of friends and
acquaintances, including politicians, lawyers, traders,
farmers, all sorts and conditions of men, excepting only
soldiers and sailors.

The Government. The President elect did not fill the
Cabinet with his own friends and personal supporters.
His one object was to keep a compact front against
secession ; all shades of Unionists, all parts of the
country, all the various interests, must be represented.
Thus the Cabinet was something of the coalition type.
Seward of New York was known to be a ' Conserva-
tive ', that is to say, a moderate ; a very able man,
he did great work as Secretary of State—a position
something like that of our Foreign Minister. Chase of
Ohio was Secretary of the Treasury ; a Radical or
' Black Republican ', sternly opposed to any compromise about slavery. Cameron of Pennsylvania represented business interests and Protection. All three
had been Lincoln's rivals at the Republican Convention ;
with much experience in statecraft they were naturally
sore that their claims had been passed over in favour
of a comparatively unknown new-comer ; small-minded
men might have found consolation in seeing their
successful rival in difficulties. Other members, though
not so prominent, had various separate interests.

It required some courage and self-confidence to
harness together a mixed team of this sort ; a heavy
hand would make them jib ; too light a hand would
mean loss of control ; it is a proof of real power and
tact in the teamster that, with the exception of
Cameron, they were kept together and pulled the
right way.

Cameron had received a promise of office, before the election, from the party managers ; it was given without Lincoln's knowledge, and it was only with reluctance that he carried it out. It is surprising, in these circumstances, that he was made Secretary for War when this office was likely to become so important. It is not surprising that in November '61 he was invited to resign. His successor was Stanton.

Though the President gave his subordinates, especially Seward and Chase, a very free hand in their own departments, he was firm on any point about which he had convictions of his own. On certain occasions he made big decisions without consulting them, and even when they disagreed with him. It is a proof of their greatness, not of their littleness or weakness, that they served him loyally, and came to recognize him as the master mind—in Seward's words, ' the best man of us all.'

And yet, while he did not interfere with other offices, Lincoln paid the closest attention to the War Department ; in the circumstances it could not be otherwise ; no order, except on routine and minor details, was issued without his approval.

This is an all-important point. At the beginning of the war the North met with terrible defeats. The critics look for somebody to hang. In some cases military critics have decided that the mistakes were caused by ' civilians ' who over-ruled professional soldiers. ' Civilians '—but, in view of Lincoln's great prestige, there is hesitation about fixing upon him as the chief criminal ; and so the blame is laid on Cameron, Stanton, or the collective Cabinet. Cameron quitted office before big operations began, and may be left out of consideration. Stanton has been selected as chief whipping-boy—' the evil genius of the North '— and comes in for very heavy abuse.

Now there is no doubt, as will be seen, that the broad

strategy was controlled from Washington. Plans were drawn up by soldiers, but Lincoln reserved to himself the power to accept or amend or reject them. From my point of view some of the alleged mistakes were not mistakes at all and therefore need no excuse. But for the moment let that pass, and admit that there were some mistakes. To shift the blame on Stanton is no excuse for Lincoln—rather is it an additional charge of weakness or indecision or carelessness. To my mind an attempt to relieve Lincoln of responsibility is the most derogatory thing that has ever been said about him.

Not that he was self-opinionated—on the contrary, he was painfully aware of his ignorance of military affairs; and, as Lord Charnwood says, he was not quick at arriving at a decision. He would examine a plan, ask questions, listen with patience to the views of other people, and on minor questions he was not insistent. But where big issues were involved he wanted to be convinced before he gave approval, and he had sufficient confidence in his own mental powers to feel that he could come to a logical decision when a problem was clearly stated.

At the outset his chief military adviser was Winfield Scott, Lieutenant-General of the Federal army—a fine old veteran who had held command in Mexico, but he was now getting on in years, too infirm for service in the field, unable even to get on a horse and carry out an inspection. He recommended as commander in the field Colonel Robert E. Lee. This officer was exactly the type of man that Lincoln was looking for. His knowledge, experience, above all his imagination, were the very qualities in which our Strategist was deficient—and knew he was deficient. Had he been available Lee would have made a perfect Von Moltke to Lincoln's Von Bismarck; Lincoln would have gladly resigned to him the responsibility as Strategist of the North, and history would have been written differently. But Lee was a Virginian, and when that State seceded he felt bound, not without misgiving, to obey her call. Of him more anon.

So General Scott stayed on as sole adviser till November '61, when he resigned. Fifty years of service had encrusted him with the routine of a small regular army, and he had not the elasticity of touch which is necessary to model large numbers of undisciplined recruits into a fighting machine. With all the will in the world he was not very resourceful or helpful.

The Outbreak of War. Mr. Buchanan, the retiring President, sent a message to Congress on the 4th December 1860, expressly denying the Right of Secession, but adding that the Federal Government had no right to coerce a seceding State. It was well known at the time that South Carolina was about to secede (the actual Ordinance of Secession was passed on the 20th December), so Buchanan's declaration, however correct from a legal point of view, was not a solution of a practical problem. This problem continued to exercise the minds of men for the next five months. But surely Lincoln must have solved it in his own mind ? We know that he had a habit of stripping a problem to its simplest form—its fundamental facts. The outstanding fact was that secession had been proclaimed—to him this was illegal. The second fact was that the seceding States had definitely declared their position to be ' thoroughly identified with slavery '—to him this was abhorrent. He had admitted the existence of slavery, but only as an evil too deeply rooted to be eradicated by violent methods ; the declaration of the South was intended to recognize it as a proper institution, worthy to be perpetuated and extended. Anything like compromise on either of these two points would mean the abandonment of his deepest convictions and a breach of his election pledges to the nation—in fact it would not be a compromise but a surrender. As there was no possibility that the Southern States would recant they must be coerced, which meant war to the bitter end.

Thus, it came that Lincoln, who of all men hated war, was the one man on whose shoulders lay the responsibility for the greatest Civil War ever known. In a sense it was not a war of his making, for he could not control the situation before March '61. In another sense it was of his making, for it was he who refused to allow the Union to be broken up and the cause of slavery to be stamped with the approval of his country.

It would be greatly interesting to know at what precise moment he recognized war as inevitable. We cannot look to his speeches for enlightenment ; in hours of crisis a statesman, like a general, cannot reveal all his thoughts and plans either to his opponents or his followers ; he must be moderate in his language, to avoid stirring up passion, and while it is not admissible to state untruths it is the statesman's licence to use a tone of optimism which his own views do not justify. As late as March Lincoln ' hoped that bloodshed would be avoided '. But his mind was so clear and his convictions so firm that I think he must have felt that war was inevitable as soon as South Carolina passed the Ordinance of Secession—this, however, is pure conjecture.

Be that as it may, as soon as the Strategist made up his mind to war he had to devote himself to consider means for carrying it through with success. From this point it is my intention to avoid politics as far as possible —that is to say, on all occasions except where they have a direct bearing on the military situation.

The Opposing Sides. During the course of the year '60 there was much dissension in the South. The

Republicans were few in number, the Democrats had split. But in '61 the question of secession brought them together again. South Carolina was joined almost at once by six other States, and later on four more followed, making eleven in all. Their population has been estimated at about five millions, with three and a half million slaves. Their new President, Jefferson Davis, was a man of much experience in administration, and was supported by many able men. Their attitude was firm and their policy clear ; they had no desire to attack the Northern States or to force their policy upon them : they wanted to be let alone.

Twenty-two States declared for the Union. Their population was something over twenty millions, with half a million negroes. But whereas the Republican party had been ' solid ' during the election, the question of secession brought out various shades of opinion, and this was a matter of real concern to the Strategist. He himself was determined to suppress the rebellion and maintain the Union, but immediate strong measures would raise an outcry about tyranny and aggression which would accentuate the differences among his own people. Therefore, even before raising an army, he must find some means of closing up the ranks of the civilian population. Not an easy task, and much too intricate for discussion here, but it so happened that among the problems inherited by the new President from his predecessor was one which was solved for him in a way that also solved many others. This was Fort Sumter.

Fort Sumter. Buchanan had stated his intention of holding on to the forts and other property of the Federal Government. As a matter of fact the Confederates occupied most of them without opposition. There was, however, one important exception. Outside Charleston, the main port of South Carolina, lay

three small forts, garrisoned by about 100 Federal
troops under Major Robert Anderson. This officer
concentrated his little detachment in Fort Sumter,
which lies on an artificial island in the centre of the
harbour. It was obviously incapable of defence unless
strongly reinforced. General Scott urged that reinforcements be sent ; but an attempt to do so might
be regarded as provocative, might indeed cause the
explosion which Buchanan was determined to avoid.
In the first volume of Ropes there is a full discussion of
the legal aspect, and an account of the comings and
goings of emissaries of the South who argued with
Buchanan on the subject. For five months the Sumter
affair attracted much attention in the press. It had
come to be accepted as a test case.

This was the immediate problem which faced
Lincoln on his inauguration. Should Sumter be held
and should it be reinforced ? On March 5th a letter
was received from Anderson in which he said his
supplies were running out, and, further, that 20,000
men would be required to hold the harbour per-
manently. This solved half the problem, for there
were not 20,000 men available. General Scott then
recommended that the garrison be withdrawn—from
the military point of view it was the only thing to be
done. But this would be a confession of weakness,
almost a recognition of the rights of the Confederacy.
There was, however, an alternative. The dispatch of
a shipload of stores was a matter of routine and could
not be called an act of war on the part of the Federals ;
at the same time any interference with the ship would
be an act of war on the part of the Confederates and
would throw on them the onus of the outbreak of
active hostilities.

So indeed it turned out. The ship sailed, but before
her arrival the Confederates began to bombard the
fort on April 12th. No casualties occurred, but the

barracks were set on fire. Anderson did not feel bound
to sacrifice the lives of his men by prolonging an impossible defence, so, having done enough for honour's
sake, he consented to evacuate the fort. After saluting
the flag of the Union he hauled it down and was
allowed to sail away.

How far this opening manœuvre was engineered by
Lincoln can only be a matter of doubt, but there can be
no doubt that it was just what the Strategist needed.
The intrinsic value of the fort was a minus quantity ;
it would have taken the whole of his army to garrison it.
But the dramatic end of it was a real asset. The
Confederates had put themselves out of court by
appealing to force. This solved all legal questions of
Constitutional Law at one stroke. The only remaining
question was whether the Federal Government should
or should not suppress an armed rebellion. There
could, of course, be no hesitation on the part of the
North in answering. And so the Strategist could get
down to the purely military situation.

It was a bad blunder on the part of Jefferson Davis.
He might himself have sent a cargo of provisions to
Anderson and invited him to remain in Sumter as
guest of the Confederacy—pending the settlement of
certain diplomatic questions between two Governments
which were not at war. This would have won sympathy
from many pacifists in the North. It would have kept
him right in the eyes of foreigners, who knew nothing
and cared less about the laws of the Constitution but
assumed that he had some legal position. Most
certainly it would have embarrassed Lincoln, who could
neither withdraw his garrison nor leave it there under
such conditions.

But apparently the bright young Confederates,
having asserted their independence, wanted to fight
somebody for it ; while the more sober ones, if they
had too much time for reflection, might wobble back

under the flag of the Union. So Davis decided that he must cut the painter, which still hung, loosely, between him and Washington, even if he left the windward position to Lincoln.

There was no declaration of war, but everybody knew what it meant.

IV

THE SITUATION

THIS book is not a history of the war. Historians establish facts by careful examination of all the evidence, much of which is only available after the war is over and the secrets of both sides can be revealed. The official records can then be compared and will be found to correct each other ; private documentary evidence gradually comes to light ; personal narratives and recollections correct reports which were written in haste.

But the commander has to solve his problems by the light of such information as may be available at the time ; it is always incomplete and often unreliable; the gift of weighing evidence and drawing correct inferences from even bad information is one of the greatest a commander can possess.

In judging a strategist we ought to discard knowledge which is acquired from history and try to put ourselves in his place.

An Appreciation. It is the duty of the Intelligence Branch of a War Office to collect during peacetime information about all countries in which there is even the remotest possibility of operations ; this deals with geography, climate, population, resources, and of course more particularly with the armed forces. When the possibility of war comes nearer this information is dug out of its pigeon-hole and a précis of it may be prepared. In military colleges this is known as an ' Appreciation of the situation ' ; no cut-and-dried form is laid down for it, but the following headings are suggested for consideration—irrelevant ones being of course left out according to circumstances.

A. Numbers and dispositions of our own forces, and the enemy's as far as known.

B. A discussion of the factors which will affect operations ; these may include :

1. Notes on geography. Natural obstacles, such as mountains, rivers, deserts, marshes. Strategical points, fortresses, arsenals, dockyards, harbours, railway junctions. Means of communication, railroads, canals, roads, bridges. Water. Supplies.

2. Physical factors (physical is a conventional term). Numbers, armament, equipment, transport (on which depends mobility).

3. Moral factors. A special note on the commander and prominent leaders of the enemy. Training, discipline, morale of officers and men.

4. Special factors. Command of the sea, politics, public opinion, resources, finance.

C. A definition of our ultimate objects and of the immediate objects that lead up to it.

D. Possible courses open to the enemy.

E. A proposal for action.

. . . .

The stock example of an Appreciation is the one compiled by Von Moltke before the Prusso-Austrian War of 1866. He finds the physical factors evenly balanced, except that the needle-gun of the Prussians would give their infantry a real advantage over the Austrians with their muzzle-loaders. He discusses the possibility of intervention on the Austrian side by Russia or France ; this leads to calculations of time and space to see how soon such intervention could appear in the field. This leads to the point that the Prussians must strike quickly. This leads to a review

of the routes running towards Vienna and the big
obstacle presented by the mountains ; as the passes
are few and far between the army must spread out very
wide in order that the leading corps may each have
a road to itself. This leads to a discussion of the risk
involved by too wide a dispersion, and fresh calculations of time and space to see how quickly concentration on the far side of the range can be secured.
He decides that the Austrian mobilization will be slow,
so the risk is not great. He has thus arrived at a definite
proposal for action.

It is an interesting document for several reasons.
It shows that a well-trained general who grasps the
initiative can make accurate forecasts and calculations.
War was declared on June 15th. The Prussians were
already mobilized and crossed the mountains in six
columns, widely spread out, the extreme wings being
over one hundred miles apart. On the far side the
right wing and centre concentrated without hindrance.
The left wing met with some opposition as it debouched
from its passes but was able to get through. It joined
hands with the rest on the decisive field of Sadowa
while the battle was actually in progress. Every corps
got up to throw its weight into a big enveloping attack.
So the Austrians were defeated by July 4th.

But the chief interest lies in the way it enables us to
trace the reasoning with which a great commander
builds up his strategy. He picks out the factors which
are in his favour and writes them down as assets ; on
the debit side he enters the factors favourable to his
opponent. By bringing his assets into full play and
neutralizing his debits he gets a balance which means
victory. Von Moltke picked out Time as the decisive
factor ; he therefore gained time by thorough organization, quick mobilization, rapid marches on several
roads, and clever use of railways. In this way he
deprived the Austrians of the use of a strong line of

mountains, and avoided the danger of what appeared to be a risky dispersal of his forces.

Now it is not to be supposed that Lincoln sat down to balance his ledger after the trained methods of the Prussian, but, of course, he studied the situation, and it is fair to assume that his review led to conclusions which may be summarized as follows.

Politics. Greater weight had to be given to political considerations than is the case in most wars, because there still remained a number of people who had not made up their minds on which side to fight. Most of these were in the border States—Virginia, Missouri, Kentucky, and Maryland.

Virginia divided into two, the eastern half as far as the Alleghanies went over to the Confederacy, while the western half declared for the Union. Such loyalty, of course, deserved support, and Western Virginia must be defended.

In Missouri there was no geographical line of cleavage, but they got up a civil war of their own. It was necessary to support the Unionists, or Missouri would be lost.

Kentucky wanted to keep out of the war altogether, and proclaimed a neutrality. But a Southern force began to move in, so a Northern one had to be sent to oppose it.

Maryland was only neutral in the sense that she sent regiments to fight on each side. As Washington lay to the south of Maryland it was all the more important that the State should be prevented from seceding.

If any one of these States went over to the Confederacy it would count two on a division, for recruits would not only be lost to the Federal ranks but would probably join the enemy. As a matter of fact, except half Virginia, they remained in the Union, but historians have not yet decided whether this was due to their convictions or to the actual presence of Union troops.

Thus, Lincoln was compelled to base his strategy on the ruling principle that Washington and the border States must be held at all costs ; this entailed leaving detachments to watch a front over 1,000 miles in length, and there was no concealment of the fact that the reasons for this were purely political.

This is a very important point, because it marks the first rift between his strategy and the orthodox faith— only a little rift as yet, but to grow into a chasm later on. The true faith is that attack is always the best means of defence, and that all forces should be concentrated to form a mass for offensive action ; this mass should be directed against the main body of the enemy. Passive resistance can never be anything but a crime. A temporary attitude of defence, with a view to counter-attack, may be condoned only on the Jesuitical principle of doing evil that good may come ; but it must be regarded with suspicion, and the counter-stroke must be prepared beforehand.

Now if this ' grand principle of warfare ' be applied to the present case it means that all the Federal forces should have been collected ; they would form a steam-roller which could crush Virginia and take Richmond ; the rebellion would then collapse ; meanwhile the border States would have to take care of themselves. ' If you cut down a tree the branches will fall.'

None of the critics has gone so far as to put this into words as a serious suggestion. They recognize that in a benighted country, where war is unknown, politics must have their say ; much may be forgiven to the heathen in his blindness. But if in this instance Lincoln was more to be pitied than blamed it was the first symptom of political interference, and he must be watched in future.

Lincoln himself was quite shrewd enough to see that

a passive defensive would guard his own States but would never crush the rebellion. He must therefore think out offensive measures of some kind.

Here he picked out as his chief asset Command of the Sea, and it was one which could be brought to bear on a weak point of the enemy. The capital of the South was locked up in plantations and slaves. There was little internal trade. Commerce, and with it finance, depended on keeping open communications with Europe. Five million bales of cotton had been shipped to England in 1860. At the same time the South was not rich in factories, and would want to draw munitions as well as other necessaries from abroad. A tight blockade would therefore cripple finance and cut off supplies: it would thus be a real offensive measure. The task was not an easy one ; Lincoln deserves credit for seeing that it could be carried out and that no expense should be grudged that would make it effective. He proclaimed the blockade on April 19th, five days after the fall of Fort Sumter. It was true strategical foresight. The total coast-line to be watched was over 3,000 miles long and contained a couple of hundred harbours.

The Blockade. In 1860 the U.S. Navy had only forty-two vessels in commission, half of them sailing ships ; but in those days, before ironclads, any merchantman could be transformed into a second-class man-of-war by putting a few light guns on board. By December 1861 there were 264 ships, and before the end of the war there were nearly 700.

Crews were recruited from the merchant service, who understood navigation and seamanship. The officers were accustomed to command and the men to discipline. Gunnery was not yet a fine art and could very soon be picked up. In the matter of personnel the navy was much better off than the army. Professor

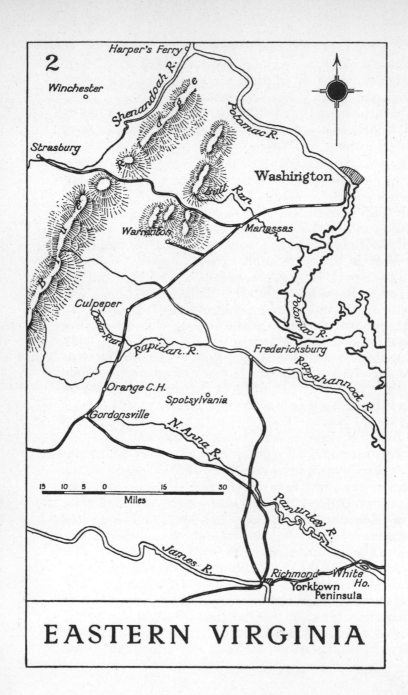

2

Harper's Ferry

Winchester

Shenandoah R.

Potomac R.

Washington

Strasburg

Bull Run

Warrenton

Manassas

Potomac R.

Culpeper

Rapidan R.

Fredericksburg

Rappahannock R.

Orange C.H.

Spotsylvania

Gordonsville

N. Anna R.

15 10 5 0 15 30
Miles

Pamunkey R.

James R.

Richmond
Yorktown
Peninsula

White
Ho.

EASTERN VIRGINIA

Paxson says : ' Every village politician believed himself competent to be a colonel, if not a brigadier-general, while the public, unaccustomed to dwell on special fitness, assumed that military capacity was inherent in all. But few fancied themselves able to command a ship, and the navy was left, generally, to the control of experts.' At their head was the Secretary, G. S. Welles, a good organizer.

The South had no navy to start with, and though a few vessels were improvised the actual fighting was confined to some duels which have attracted attention as romantic incidents. The real business was done by the blockade.

But, though sure, the blockade must take a long time to exert real pressure. The South, rich in food supplies, could maintain itself for a time, and it was only by degrees that the pinch was felt. And the scope of a navy is confined to the seas and the coast ; the army of the South was as safe from the navy of the North as an elephant is from a whale. So, though the blockade was the main offensive, something must also be done on land if the rebellion was to be suppressed soon.

Land Operations. This brings us down to the scene of the campaigns.

A glance at the map shows that the range of the Alleghanies cuts the country into two, so, as might be expected, there were two distinct theatres of war.

A. The Western Theatre, its main features being the great rivers Ohio and Mississippi.

B. The Eastern Theatre, chiefly in Virginia. This was the more important from the fact that it contained both the capitals—Washington and Richmond. The main armies would naturally be found either defending their own capital or threatening that of the enemy.

The division between the two theatres was so complete that operations in the one had little direct bearing on the other. This simplifies the narrative; attention can be concentrated on the East right up till July 1863, after which the story of the West can follow.

Numbers. At the outbreak of war the standing army of the United States numbered about 16,000 officers and men. Nearly all the men remained loyal to the Union, but most of them were scattered in the small forts which guarded the Indian frontier, and only 3,000 were available for service in the East. There were about 1,200 officers who had been trained at West Point ; about one-third of these were Southerners, and, with few exceptions, they resigned their commissions and joined the army of the South.

Immediately after the fall of Fort Sumter the President issued proclamations calling for the following recruits :

Volunteers for three months' service . . .	75,000
Volunteers for three years' service	42,000
Recruits for the Regular Army	22,000
Recruits for the Navy	18,000
Total .	157,000

At first sight it looks like an error of judgement to have fixed so short a period as three months for any of the volunteers—an indication that Lincoln had very little idea of the task in front of him—in fact, a great lack of the foresight which is the first requisite in a strategist. It must, however, be noted that the appeal was made by Lincoln on his own responsibility, without consulting Congress, and as the President has no right to declare war or raise troops without the assent of Congress, he was stretching his powers quite as far if not farther than the limits intended by the Constitution. At the same time an extra session of Congress was summoned for July 4th, and as soon as it met the President sent a message asking for confirmation of his action and further power to raise the total to 400,000.

It seems that Lincoln did not want to fluster the nation, and especially the doubtful States ; the call to arms must be posted in every village, and an appeal on too large a scale would give a handle to discontent, arouse alarm, and deter waverers. On the whole it appears that Lincoln himself saw a long way ahead, but did not consider the nation was yet fit to be taken into full confidence.

The system of recruiting was through the Governors of the various States. The President called on each State to supply a certain quota of the total required ; the Governor then made his own arrangements for enrolling and collecting recruits. At first there was little difficulty, but later on, when the demands increased, there was a good deal of jealousy and the system did not work smoothly.

The call for recruits was oversubscribed, and 90,000 were accepted. Many, however, were absorbed in garrisons, and it was only by degrees that a surplus of 50,000 could be collected near Washington for offensive measures.

This force was divided into two. At Washington General McDowell had 35,000, organized in five divisions (Tyler, Hunter, Heintzleman, Runyon, Miles).

At Harper's Ferry, fifty miles to the north-west, was a detachment of 15,000 under General Patterson.

Reports showed that the enemy had also two forces, about 20,000 under Beauregard covering the important railway junction at Manassas ; about 10,000 under J. E. Johnston facing Patterson. (See sketch 3.)

Armament. Both sides had muzzle-loading rifles, sighted up to 1,000 yards. The North had also rifled guns, which gave them an advantage over the Southern artillery which had only smooth-bores.

Transport was all improvised. As a rule it was sufficient and of fair material, but the drivers were unorganized and undisciplined, so it was unwieldy and difficult to manage.

Moral Factors. It was recognized that the South had the better raw material for their ranks—hunters, trappers, farmers, most of them able to ride and use the rifle. Many of the Northerners came from offices and shops and were not accustomed to outdoor life.

Discipline did not exist on either side ; the men had never been brought up to it. ' Waterloo was won on the playing fields of Eton '—which means that the boys began early to grasp the principles of team-work and leadership, of obedience and command. Few of the Americans had been through the discipline of a regular school or university. They could not be brought to see that it was not theirs to reason why. Mere rank did not inspire respect. There were many born leaders among them, but they had to win the confidence of their followers ; it was not ready-made. Regular officers of the European school would have been driven to fury or despair, but the American officers, brought up in the same way as their men, kept their tempers and made the best they could of it.

And yet this independence, which would have brought half of them to court martial in the Prussian army, produced self-reliance and initiative far above that of any machine-made force. Nobody waited for orders if an opportunity were seen ; scouting was bold and intelligent ; in fact, all the individual work was good. But team-work was poor, and the manœuvre of masses was bad ; for this, however, the untrained staff must share the blame.

The Northerners were by no means inferior in brains and education ; they had as good drill-instructors as the enemy. There was no reason why they should not train into good soldiers.

The skill of the opposing generals was as yet an

unknown factor. Staff-work was so little understood
that the lack of it was not realized till later on.

Training. Scott and McDowell both reported that
the training was incomplete. It was not, however, a
question of the army being good or bad, but of its
relative value compared with the enemy. If the North
wanted more time to organize and train, the South
wanted it too.

To sum up. As far as could be seen the factors were
evenly balanced except that the Federals had a superiority in numbers, about 50,000 against 30,000 ; this was
sufficient to decide Lincoln on an advance. It is as
certain as anything can be that if he had held on without
attacking he would have been condemned for throwing
away a golden opportunity.

It has been said that popular clamour influenced his
decision. This I do not believe. It is true that the
recruits were tired of the parade ground and wanted to
take the field : Congress was sitting and, having made
up its mind that the rebellion would collapse at the
first blow, wanted to get on with it : the press and the
populace were certainly clamouring for ' something to
be done '. A weak man might have felt the pressure—
but Lincoln was not weak, least of all when the lives
of Americans came into the question. If, in his
opinion, the military situation showed a balance in his
favour then he was justified—in fact he was bound to
act as he did. If, on the other hand, he considered that
the odds were against him, if he acted only as the
result of popular clamour—it was a crime.

My view is that the Strategist was influenced only by
military considerations, but the Statesman allowed his
politicians to think that they had some influence : it
costs little to ' defer ' to another man's opinion when
that opinion happens to coincide exactly with your own :
the Statesman was still busy keeping his own team

together. This is, of course, a pure conjecture, and scarcely fits in with the usual downright methods of ' honest Abe ' ; if it is too far-fetched I revert to the simpler view, that he acted on military reasonings and must take the credit or the blame.

Dispositions. At the beginning of July the information was fairly correct. The dispositions were roughly as shown on sketch 3, Beauregard could be outnumbered unless he were reinforced by Johnston. To prevent such reinforcement Patterson was ordered to move southwards and occupy the attention of Johnston, in the Shenandoah Valley, but without committing himself to a general engagement. This sounds simple, but is really one of the most difficult tasks in war. With a small mobile body the enemy can be harassed and threatened—later on Stonewall Jackson showed himself a master of such tactics. But Patterson's force was not sufficiently trained, nor well enough staffed, for such delicate work. He pushed southwards on July 2nd, and some skirmishing took place in the next few days. His reports showed that he was in close touch with Johnston, and therefore it was taken for granted that a sharp advance by McDowell would catch Beauregard unsupported. On July 11th and 13th McClellan defeated a Southern force in Western Virginia. The moment seemed therefore to have arrived for McDowell to advance. He left Washington on July 16th.

MARCHES TO FIRST BULL RUN

Strength of Forces

Patterson : 15,000   Mc Dowell : 35,000
Johnston : 11,000   Beauregard : 22,000

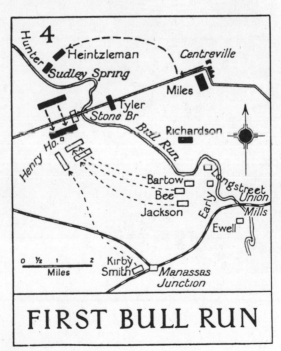

FIRST BULL RUN

IRVIN MCDOWELL (1818–1885)
Major General, U.S.A.

V

FIRST BULL RUN

AS this essay is concerned with strategy it is not necessary to consider the tactics in full detail. The battle fought on July 21st is known as First Bull Run because a second one was fought on the same ground next year. In the South it is generally known as First Manassas.

McDowell left Washington on the afternoon of July 16th. It was only about thirty miles to Bull Run, but the weather was oppressively hot, the men straggled badly, and it was not till the evening of the 20th that they were formed up, ready for attack on the next day.

For some time the Confederates had been expecting his advance and admirable plans had been prepared to meet it. Johnston was to leave a skeleton force under Stuart to keep Patterson amused, while his main body slipped away : by forced marching (twenty-six miles) they were to reach Piedmont, on the railway : there the infantry was to take train to Manassas Junction, thus avoiding thirty miles by road and gaining at least two days.

It speaks well for the secrecy of the Federal plans that no definite information about the advance leaked out until McDowell was actually on the road. It was only at 1 a.m. on the 18th that Johnston heard of it ; he moved at once ; the infantry reached Piedmont on the 19th and began to entrain. But it had been impossible to collect enough rolling stock to carry them all, so by the 20th only three brigades (Bee, Bartow, and Jackson), together with the cavalry and artillery, had joined Beauregard. Kirby Smith's brigade did not arrive till the afternoon of the 21st—the day of the battle.

51

Beauregard's position was on the west bank of the Bull Run (see sketch 4) ; this stream could be crossed at several bridges and fords, but its steep wooded banks made it a formidable obstacle to a frontal attack. McDowell at first thought of turning the position from the south, but the roads on that side were bad, so he decided to move round the other flank. His reserve was left at Centreville : a detaining force was posted opposite the Confederate front : the divisions of Hunter and Heintzleman were sent right round to Sudley Springs, to make the main attack : Tyler's division was directed to the Stone Bridge, to act as a connecting link and to come in as opportunity presented itself.

The plan was good, but the Staff failed to keep the roads clear and there was much delay. It was only some six miles to Sudley Springs, but the Federals took nearly as many hours to get there. By 9 a.m. the two divisions had formed up on the west bank and began their advance southwards.

The Confederates had meanwhile observed the turning movement and were sending troops to meet it. The Federals pushed steadily forward for a couple of miles and reached the Henry House Hill, where the decisive struggle took place. The Confederate brigades of Bee and Bartow put up an obstinate defence, but were forced to give ground, and it looked as if the Federals had won the day.

About noon Jackson's brigade arrived and took up a position behind which the broken Confederates could re-form. It was at this moment that Bee, who was trying to collect his men, cried to them—' Look ! there is Jackson standing like a stone wall ! Rally behind the Virginians ! ' These words gave Jackson the name which has clung to him in history.

But the Federals, after their first success, had to re-form their ranks before pressing home the advantage:

when their attack was renewed it was by successive brigades, those in rear waiting till those in front had been defeated. For three hours the fighting was very severe. Bee and Bartow were killed and their brigades were badly shattered. Stonewall Jackson was wounded in the hand, but his brigade was able to hold on grimly to its position.

Till 3 p.m. victory hung in the balance. Then Kirby Smith's brigade arrived from the railway and attacked the Federal right flank. The Northerners were too exhausted to stand against this body of fresh troops. Beauregard seized the opportunity to order a general counter-stroke—which was carried out with fine spirit and decided the day in favour of the South.

By 4 p.m. the Federals were in full retreat. The volunteers soon lost all semblance of order, and vivid descriptions have been written of the ' disgraceful rout ' and the ' terrified rabble '. One battalion of regulars kept its ranks and checked the pursuing cavalry—but there was no general pursuit.

About 18,000 men had been actually engaged on each side. The Southern casualties were 387 killed and 1,582 wounded. The North lost 460 killed, 1,124 wounded ; also 1,500 prisoners, 25 guns, and many wagons and supplies.

.   .   .   .

The Verdict. Perhaps more nonsense has been written about First Bull Run than about any other battle in history. Most of it, however, is honest nonsense, arising from the fact that the authors had no standard by which to measure what they saw and heard. A man who has never seen the ocean looks upon a duckpond as a big lot of water. The Americans had never seen war ; the long struggle against the Red Indians was a series of intermittent skirmishes : the Mexican war had been fought on foreign soil. Their idea of an army was a body of men in the precise lines of the parade ground—smart uniforms—something debonair and gay. Such was the scene on July 16th as the regiments swung past the President with bands playing and colours flying. Senators in carriages, ladies waving the Stars and Stripes, journalists thinking out superlatives for their descriptions of the coming victory.

Within a week scattered fragments came limping back, dirty and dishevelled, bringing wild tales of a stricken field.

In the course of the next few years the nation learnt what these things mean, and that even a victorious army is not a pretty sight ; they could look upon such scenes with distress, of course, but without panic ; they could wait to hear the truth before calling it a disgraceful rout and rushing into judgement. But in July '61 the shock was sudden and staggering. The people who had been loudest in clamouring for an advance now told each other about the warnings of Scott and McDowell : the Government had sent half-trained boys on an impossible task : the result was, of course, disaster : the rout was disgraceful : a bad case of political disregard of professional advice. And as such it is written down in History.

Now it was sadly true that the North had lost an important battle, but a battle may be lost by a very small margin which brings no disgrace to the losers. The critics, when looking for somebody to hang, should begin by looking for the real cause of the defeat. A bad plan means bad men at the head of affairs ; bad fighting means bad troops.

In the opening moves the Confederates scored the first point by the clever transference of Johnston to support Beauregard. But McDowell scored on the 21st by taking the initiative and turning the Confederates' flank. The first attack of the Federals was well carried out, and proves that the troops had some power of manœuvre. From noon onwards their attacks became ragged—' piecemeal '.

This brings us to some nonsense written by people who ought to have known better ; having made up their minds that the Federals could do no right they seize on the ' piecemeal attack ' as an example of crime. But chapter and verse can be quoted from Napoleon himself in favour of successive attacks. At Waterloo he made no less than five quite separate efforts—(1) preliminary attack on Hougoumont by Reille's Corps at noon ; (2) main attack from the right by D'Erlon's Corps at 1.30 ; (3) cavalry attack from the left centre at 4; (4) second attack by D'Erlon from the centre at 6; (5) final attack from the left centre by the Imperial Guard at 7. His tactics were based on the principle of keeping heavy reserves in hand ; preliminary attacks were made to deceive the enemy, draw his reserves into action, waste his ammunition ; then the French reserves were thrown in to clinch matters by the impetus of a *fresh* body at the decisive point.

In theory Von Moltke was in favour of simultaneous attacks all along the line and round the flanks. But in practice the Prussians, even with their well-trained staff, failed to carry out the idea. At Sadowa the four corps on the left only arrived after the rest of the army had been five hours in action. At Worth and Spicheren the leading divisions attacked as soon as they met the enemy, and the successive ones were thrown in as they came up.

It is hard to say what McDowell's own intention was, but what actually happened is clear enough. The commanders in the front line saw the enemy in confusion and apparently defeated ; their own men had to be re-formed, but as soon as anybody could collect a brigade, or even a battalion, he pushed forward to keep up the pressure. Hence the ' piecemeal '. It might have been better to wait till the various units

were ready to make simultaneous attacks ; but the
Confederates would have been glad to be given time,
so this must remain a matter of opinion. At worst the
' piecemeal ' was injudicious, but it certainly was not
an inexcusable crime.

In any case the Federals held the upper hand till
well past midday. Henderson gives Stonewall Jackson
and his brigade credit for turning the tide in favour of the
South—and, indeed, they earned undying glory. Other
writers give rather more weight to the arrival of Kirby
Smith and his fresh men. I suggest, however, that the
Federals were really defeated by their own exhaustion.

Physical fitness is a tremendous factor in war. It is,
of course, obvious that the army which marches best
can manœuvre best, but, in addition to this, fitness
adds that little bit of vigour at the critical hour which
weary and footsore men, however gallant, cannot
achieve. The cry is always for fresh troops—not
because the others are defeated or dismayed, but
because there is a limit to human endurance. In such
cases the troops on the defensive have a real advantage
in the simple fact that they have less marching to do.

The difference between walking and marching can
only be realized by those who have tried both. An
average healthy man thinks little of walking fifteen
miles a day if he is not hurried : when the weather is
hot he chooses the cool hours : he goes his own pace,
picks the best part of the road, takes a breather at the
top of a steep hill, and a longer rest when he needs it.
But marching is quite another thing. To begin with
he must carry rifle, ammunition, and knapsack, which
may weigh up to 50 lb. : [1] this weight shifts the balance
of the body and brings new muscles into play : the

---

[1] At the beginning of the Great War a British private carried 59 lb.
of which 10 lb. was ordinary clothing ; the rest included rifle, ammunition, bayonet, greatcoat, haversack, water-bottle, half a day's ration,
one day's emergency ration. Blanket, when carried, was an additional
4½ lb.

straps and buckles gall shoulders unaccustomed to them: pace must be suited to that of the unit, and in a long column there are constant irritating checks which always seem to come at the wrong place : it is impossible to avoid dust, mud, ruts : a new pair of regulation boots probably add torture.

The man who walks fifteen miles will scarcely march half a dozen at his first attempt, but though this may seem surprising still more wonderful is the improvement which comes with practice. Start the recruits on a progressive course of marching, suited to their physique : they very soon shake down into their boots and accoutrements : in a couple of months, given fair conditions, they will be able to do fifteen miles, and twenty at a pinch.

Now, suppose the Federals had been capable of twelve miles a day. Leaving Washington on the 16th they could have formed up on the evening of the 18th, ready to attack next morning. By that time none of Johnston's troops had reached Beauregard, and the latter would have been forced either to give up his position and uncover Manassas or else to stand and fight at a heavy disadvantage.

Leaving this out and coming to the day of the battle : the critical moment was about noon ; after that the attack lost its sting and dash. If the 18,000 men on the spot had each been fit for one more hour of vigorous work the Confederates might well have been defeated before Kirby Smith came up. And history would have been written differently.

Want of fitness spoilt the opening move, lost the battle, and finally made disorder inevitable in the retreat. It was not panic that led to the confusion, but inability to remain in the ranks ; officers could not keep their companies together because the footsore men limped along each at his own pace. One battalion of regulars kept its ranks, and many authors have pointed to this as a sign of discipline; it is equally possible that it was due to the fact that the men were accustomed to marching. The volunteers would have been willing enough to keep in the ranks had they been able to do so. But in the circumstances the maintenance of order would have been the greatest war miracle since the Walls of Jericho.

If it be accepted that lack of fitness turned the scale it follows that the blame lies with those who were responsible for the training. Scott and McDowell had been in Mexico and had seen an army on the march, so they ought to have recognized the weak point and taken steps to remedy it. It is true that they protested that the troops were unfit, but the fact that they could not march even ten miles a day reflects only on the generals themselves who controlled the training.

So much for the disorder—there remains the question of ' disgrace '. No doubt there were individuals who behaved badly—such are found in every army—but all this was highly magnified by the circumstance that they straggled back to the town and came under the eyes of journalists, street loafers, and the rest of the population; of course the story lost nothing in the telling.

In this respect the Southerners were more lucky; nobody saw them as they lay down on the field to take the rest they needed. Their own commander, Johnston, wrote, ' Our army was more disorganized by victory than that of the United States by defeat.' Coming from an experienced regular officer these words are very significant.

The same words supply the answer to more nonsense that has been written about the failure of the Southerners to follow up their success. ' The Confederates could have walked into Washington '—it seems so obvious that, when an enemy is beaten and thrown into disorder, the proper thing is to press him close and allow him no time for rest.

' Immediate pursuit ' is a principle of warfare which Napoleon preached but could not practise : even after smashing victories like Austerlitz and Jena his army of veterans required a breather and could not keep up immediate touch. Nor have other armies shown the power to do it ; the Prussians won victories at Sadowa and Worth but let the enemy slip away ; it was only when the French were surrounded at Sedan that victory was completed on the spot. In fact, among battles of the front rank Waterloo provides the single example of immediate pursuit, thorough and relentless, carried on for twenty miles ; but in this case it was possible only because two *fresh* corps of Prussians arrived on the field just as the French were breaking.

Stonewall Jackson, whose personal energy never flagged, saw with bitterness the golden opportunity fading away ; but while the surgeon was dressing his wound his words were ' Give me 10,000 fresh troops and I would be in Washington to-morrow ! ' *Fresh* troops—that was the rub : such men did not exist on the evening of July 21st.

The testimony of Johnston and Jackson proves that the Federals had given as good as they got, and helps to establish some points which may be summed up as follows.

1. Lincoln was justified in insisting on the advance. The plans were good, but were spoilt by bad execution.

2. The Federals could not march ten miles a day. This lost them the battle.

3. The blame lies with the senior officers who superintended the training and ought to have detected this weak point.

4. The same weakness led to disorder in the retreat.

A Cause of War. The Confederates remained in position at Bull Run, and the Federals assembled for the defence of Washington, so there was no big material gain or loss. The moral effect was much greater.

The causes of the war have already been discussed, and it is rather late to revert to them now ; to say that the battle of Bull Run caused the war appears to be mixing up cause and effect—like the Irishman who explained that he got drunk because he fell into a bog. Yet, if not a cause of war, Bull Run was the cause of warlike spirit. The press had been pointing to the 90,000 recruits as a proof of the enthusiasm of the country. But they only proved the call of the blood. Unfurl a banner in America (or England), tell the youths that they can leave the routine of office, shop, or plough, and enlist for three months of adventure and glory—without waiting to know more about it there will be plenty of recruits ; small boys will cheer ; young women will look on with shining eyes ; a band playing martial airs in the background completes the scene of enthusiasm. This is not meant as a sneer—we need a tonic of this sort now and then ; plenty of good red blood runs in the veins, but it grows sluggish at times and needs enthusiasm to warm up the circulation. It did not follow, however, that the Northerners wanted war ; the Abolitionists would have liked to avoid it ; the moderates were sick at the thought of a fratricidal struggle ; some people were prepared to let the Southern States go—'and a good riddance too'. To the last moment everybody prayed for peace.

But they are a proud race, these Americans, too proud to shut their eyes to defeat—indeed, they made it out worse than it really was. Then, having drained the cup of their humiliation, they got up again.

They were still praying for peace, but it must be peace with honour, so they added a proviso that they would like a victory first. This was not a longing for vengeance ; it was a passionate desire to re-establish their own self-respect.

First, of course, the soldiers themselves. The baptism of fire shakes the nerves of all men and leaves a feeling of shame which can only be wiped away by the exultation of victory. But if defeat had broken their ranks it had not broken their hearts—in fact it made the red blood run all the stronger. There was no more enlistment for three months—three years formed the period, and training was taken seriously. The lesson had been bitter but salutary, and they meant to teach the ' rebs ' a lesson some day.

So also the nation. The original causes of the war fell into the background. The only fact now remaining was that the rebels were under arms and had won the first trick. Sober men who had smiled at the early enthusiasm now enlisted themselves for three years. Women sat down to make bandages instead of flags.

Is it an exaggeration to say that Bull Run was the cause of the war in the hearts of the nation ?

Be that as it may, the results of the battle played into the hands of Lincoln. After the first shock he must have felt that defeat was not without compensation. The burden of internal discord was lifted from his shoulders for the moment. He could start work on a fresh appreciation and add to his list of assets the determination of twenty million people.

VI

ALL QUIET ON THE POTOMAC

The Lull in Operations.

IN the South the battle of Bull Run had effects both good and bad. The troops were naturally exultant, and gained a feeling of confidence in their leaders and in themselves which was of immense value throughout the war. At the same time, however, it led the politicians to false hopes that Europe would recognize the Confederacy and help them to resist the blockade.

At the outset Lincoln had refused to admit a state of war ; he argued that as it takes two people to make a quarrel, so it takes two nations to make a war ; the Americans formed one nation under one Government, and, therefore, the action of the Southern States was merely an insurrection, admittedly on a large scale and requiring something more than a police force to subdue it ; still it was a domestic affair.

There were certain advantages in taking this line. The President cannot make war without a declaration by Congress, but he can take strong action to suppress a revolt. He had no wish to have the matter thrashed out in full debate : there were political opponents who would make the most of such a chance. The Democrats who had been disunited might rally to oppose him ; the Abolitionists might demand a declaration about emancipation ; the big issue of the Union might be smothered in minor questions ; in any case a debate would accentuate and expose the differences among the Unionists. This he was determined to avoid.

Secondly, he did not want foreign nations officially to

recognize the Confederacy. If they did so President Davis would have the right to send his own Ministers to the Courts of Europe, and Lincoln saw the trouble that would follow. By maintaining the theory of 'domestic insurrection' he hoped that 'foreign nations, like friendly and discreet neighbours, would remain blind and deaf to it '. The theory was in accordance with Constitutional Law, and, as Professor Paxson says, was entitled to respect as long as the United States acted upon it. But Lincoln himself was the first to break away—in declaring a blockade. A British blockade-runner was seized and taken into port ; if war existed such action was justifiable ; but if the United States were ' at peace ' this was a violation of the rights of a friendly nation. The Supreme Court in trying the case took the view that war existed : ' The resistance and the powers needed to suppress it went beyond the incidents of mob violence and became a war ; the President was bound to meet it in the shape that it presented itself without waiting for Congress to baptize it with a name ; and no name given it by him or them could change the fact.'

If, however, his action was in theory inconsistent, in practice it turned out wisely ; and the wisest part of it was the selection of Charles F. Adams as Minister in London. This gentleman, elderly, calm, and honest, soon won the respect of Lord John Russell, the British Foreign Minister, and though there were moments of severe tension he always received a polite if not sympathetic hearing. It seems to have been due to the patience and wisdom of Adams that Great Britain never gave official recognition to the South, and yet accepted the blockade as a fact. This was exactly what Lincoln wanted.

The ' Trent ' Case. The greatest tension was felt in December '61. Early in the year the Confederates had sent agents to sound the Courts of Europe and to order munitions and stores. After the success at Bull Run President Davis decided to send two special emissaries, John Slidell and James Mason.

These two succeeded in slipping through the blockade and reached Havana; there they took passage in the British mail-packet *Trent* bound for Southampton. On November 8th the ship was met by the U.S. gunboat *San Jacinta*, Captain Wilkes; this officer fired a shot across the bows of the British ship, then took a boarding party and arrested the two Ministers with their secretaries. The *Trent* was allowed to proceed on her way, while the prisoners were taken to Boston and confined. This feat was hailed with delight by the people of the North, who had not yet had any success to arouse their enthusiasm; Captain Wilkes was greeted with dinners and presentation swords, and became the popular hero of the day.

This arrest on a neutral ship was not without precedent; during the Napoleonic wars the British Navy had never waited to argue about International Law when there was a seizure to be made. But the mere fact of the arrest was enough to stir the British nation to an extent which no Government could afford to disregard, and we were faced with the situation of the Mother Country intervening in a quarrel between the two prodigal but unrepentant sons who had left her side nearly a century earlier.

The British Minister in Washington was instructed to demand the release of the prisoners. The Union Government saw that if this was refused it would mean, if not war, at least the recognition of the South—which was to be avoided at all costs. The prisoners were released, and the Government without censuring Wilkes disavowed his action.

But public feeling on both sides of the Atlantic was much excited; the incident still rankled with the

British and was very useful to those who were spreading the propaganda of the South ; while in the North there was much disgust over giving up their prisoners.

It was probably the hope of the intervention of England which held the Confederates from following up their first success. President Davis wished to emphasize that the attitude of the South was not aggressive. A council of war was held in October '61 which was attended by the leading generals ; they were in favour of offensive action before the North could train a new army ; the President, however, rejected their proposals, and until March '62 there were no operations in Eastern Virginia.

Preparations. It is an axiom of military science that an Appreciation can only look as far as the next big battle. The result of this will change many factors ; the positions of the armies must be altered ; there is some gain of morale on one side and a corresponding loss on the other. So the strategist must take fresh stock of his assets and liabilities before deciding on future plans.

Napoleon always insisted strongly on preparation before a campaign, and Von Moltke was even more elaborate in his schemes. Their men were trained, their guns were ready, and it only remained to set the armies in motion ; as a rule campaigns were sharp and decisive.

In Anglo-Saxon countries there is none of this. Previous preparation demands much expenditure, and a Government which proposed any big measures in peace time would cease to be a Government. But after the shock of the first disaster preparation becomes a patriotic duty and a vote-catching proposition, so it is taken in hand with much energy. We have had to introduce the term ' current preparation ', which sounds Irish but is essentially Anglo-Saxon.

Before making fresh plans Lincoln had to find a fresh

army. There was, however, little difficulty in this ; recruits came in faster than they could be trained, and the whole thing was a matter of organization. In this he was much helped by General McClellan. By December there were 170,000 men, well armed and equipped. The time had come to consider plans.

The Great Controversy. In order to get a clear view of the controversy which arose between Lincoln and McClellan it is as well to anticipate events very briefly.

McClellan proposed to move his main body round by sea to the Yorktown peninsula for an advance on Richmond. Lincoln agreed, on the condition that sufficient force should be left to defend Washington and Maryland. McClellan intended to take about 150,000 men on his expedition, and had actually started with 108,000 when Lincoln was informed that insufficient forces had been left for the stipulated defence. Thereupon he detained one corps which was about to embark. McClellan delayed his attack on Richmond, demanding reinforcements. This gave the Confederates time to make another brilliant concentration, as they had done at Bull Run. The result was the defeat of the Peninsular campaign. Lincoln's action has given rise to furious criticism. Lord Wolseley is the most outspoken, and calls it ' the notorious instance of Mr. Lincoln's interference.' . . . ' in my opinion if McClellan had not been interfered with by the Cabinet he would probably have succeeded '. . . . ' the best way of defending Washington was to give McClellan means of advancing rapidly on Richmond.'

These are serious charges, and must be considered in detail.

The Army of the Potomac. Though General George McClellan was not yet thirty-five years of age, his career showed signs of much promise. He passed out of the Military Academy first of his class, and then went through the Mexican War with distinction, earning the brevet of captain. After spending three years as an instructor of engineering at West Point he did some survey work for new railroads. In 1854 he was selected to go to the Crimea and study the British and French armies. When he returned to America he was tempted to resign his commission and take up railway engineering. Promotion came quickly, and in 1860 he accepted the Presidency of the Ohio and Mississippi Railroad, with head-quarters at Cincinnati, where he settled down with a charming bride.

At the outbreak of war he was appointed to a command which included Western Virginia. There he gained a couple of cheap successes. After Bull Run General Scott recommended that he should be given the command at Washington.

From the moment of his arrival in the Capital, McClellan set to work, first to organize the defences of the city, and after that to train an army for offensive operations. In the course of a month forts were thrown up round Washington, separate works with a perimeter of thirty-three miles. The new recruits began their training in camps on the north side, and were afterwards sent over to the Virginian side, where they were formed into brigades and divisions. In August McClellan submitted a confidential scheme for an advance through Manassas on Richmond; but for this he required 270,000 men, and of course they could not be found at once. Seeing the energy that was displayed, the country was at first patient and content. But towards November the murmur arose again about the delay in active operations.

McClellan was in a difficult position. He had no intention of repeating the fiasco of Bull Run, but by the time his men were ready to take the field the winter had set in and the roads were unfit for an army. It seems that from the first he intended to wait for the spring, and it is generally admitted that this was wise. But of course he could not announce such an intention. If the Confederates learnt that they would not be attacked their troops at Manassas could be transferred to the West, where they were badly wanted. To deceive the enemy McClellan must also deceive his own people—and this was certainly the first cause of public discontent—unfair, but not unnatural. The daily bulletin ' All quiet on the Potomac ', which had been received with relief in August, began to cause amusement in October, and finally was hailed with derision.

On November 1st General Scott resigned and McClellan succeeded him as Commander of all the forces of the Union.

In December the young general fell ill and was unable to attend to business till January 12th. As soon as he recovered Lincoln pressed him to produce a plan, and on the 27th issued a formal order that the advance should be begun on February 22nd.

McClellan's Appreciation.   In the middle of March there were 230,000 men available in Eastern Virginia. They had all been in camp for over three months ; they were well equipped and in good condition. Brigades and divisions were organized under generals who had been carefully selected and had got to know their men. Discipline was improving, though there was still much absence, with or without leave, which reduced the effective numbers. The morale was excellent, and the whole army showed confidence in its commander.

The main body of the enemy lay in a strongly entrenched position at Manassas, supplied by a railway which ran directly to the rear and was therefore well covered. McClellan had entrusted to a firm of de-

tectives the duty of collecting intelligence regarding
the numbers opposed to him ; this was perhaps the
best that could be done ; but the reports should have
been carefully sifted and collated by a trained officer,
which apparently was not done. The information
was of course secret, and no detail has even been
published. The estimate came to 100,000 men at
Manassas and 15,000 in the Shenandoah Valley. There
is no doubt that McClellan honestly believed these
numbers to be correct, and therefore they must be
accepted for the purpose of appreciation.

The next factor of importance was geography—or,
to put it more shortly, mud. Napoleon said of Poland:
' Dieu, outre l'eau, l'air, la terre, et le feu, a créé
un cinquième élément, la boue.' McClellan said the
same of Eastern Virginia, and as regards the winter
months, this was correct. The Old Dominion which
lies between Washington and Richmond consists of
a hundred miles of mud ; rivers which in wet weather
are unfordable ; countless creeks and streams ; thick
forests ; no towns which could shelter more than a
handful of men. Two lines of railway lead to Richmond : one from Fredericksburg, 60 miles ; the other
from Alexandria (opposite Washington) by way of
Gordonsville, 130 miles. But the enemy would be
sure to remove rolling stock, demolish bridges, and tear
up the permanent way ; it might take months to
repair them. By keeping farther inland firmer ground
could be found, but only in the mountainous country.
An advance by the Shenandoah Valley was out of the
question ; there were only two roads, one of them
good but quite insufficient for a large army ; and the
southern end of the Valley was still 100 miles from
Richmond.

In fact Eastern Virginia was as bad a stretch of
country as could be found for operations, and any
plan must be a choice of evils.

Alternative Plans. Four different lines of advance were discussed.

1. A direct advance by Manassas. Lincoln preferred this route. It kept the army between the enemy and Washington. But it involved an attack on an entrenched position, and, if this were successful, a further advance over mud.

2. By water to Acquia Creek, and thence by Fredericksburg. This plan found no favour and need not be discussed at present.

3. By water to Urbana and thence to Richmond (fifty miles).

4. By water to Fort Monroe, and thence up the Yorktown peninsula. Supplies could afterwards be sent to West Point, which is only thirty miles from Richmond.

McClellan preferred the Urbana route (No. 3). He asserted that the roads in that direction were good at all times of the year, which shows that he was very badly informed, for the reverse is the truth. Furthermore, Urbana was a bad landing-place. Lincoln refused to consider this scheme, and in the end he gave his general the choice between Nos. 1 and 4. McClellan says, ' Of course I chose the latter.'

The discussion was dragged out for some time, and before it was finally settled two events occurred to alter the situation.

The ' Merrimac '. The Federals had abandoned the naval dockyard at Norfolk in April '61. The Confederates raised a wooden frigate which had been sunk there, fitted her with armour-plating, and christened her the *Merrimac*. On March 8th she appeared off Fort Monroe and had no difficulty in sinking a couple of Federal ships. Next day, however, she was challenged by the *Monitor*. This ship was another experiment in naval construction ; her sides were cut down to the water-line, and on an armoured deck there was one heavily plated turret. Though quite unseaworthy, she managed to creep down to Fort Monroe. On March 9th the famous duel took place between the two ironclads; for a couple of hours they pounded each other at close range, but without serious effect; then the *Merrimac* sheered off and made her way back to Norfolk.

The Confederates Retire. On the same date, March 9th, the Confederates disappeared southwards from Manassas. The natural inference was that they had got wind of the Fort Monroe scheme and were therefore withdrawing their main body for the defence of Richmond.

It is hard to conceive how McClellan can ever have had hopes of effecting a surprise. In Maryland there were many sympathizers with the South, including, no doubt, professional spies. The movement of 150,000 men by sea demands a large number of vessels; the business of hiring and collecting them was begun in February. It was the height of optimism to expect that so great a movement would escape observation. The Confederates could not and did not know the date of departure or the intended point of disembarkation; but, given the fact that a large force was going somewhere by sea, it required no great calculation to foresee that it was intended for an attack on Richmond. At all events the withdrawal of the Southern army dispelled any hope of finding Richmond ungarrisoned, and McClellan had to face the probability of meeting the full strength of the South whichever route he took.

In spite of this he clung to his scheme. On March 13th a council of war was held, consisting of the four corps commanders—McDowell, Sumner, Heintzleman, and Keyes. These officers voted in favour of the Fort Monroe plan, provided that 'the force to be left to cover Washington be such as to give an entire feeling of security for its safety from menace'. This force was estimated at 35,000 men, with an additional 25,000 to cover the line of the Potomac.

Lincoln reluctantly agreed. Instinct told him that the plan was unsound, but he was quite aware of his own ignorance of military matters, and he felt that he could not override the opinion of the four senior officers whom he himself had appointed. On the same day the Secretary for War informed McClellan officially that his scheme was approved.

The Fort Monroe Plan. The critics are very much divided in opinion about the movement by sea. Ropes is strongly against it and puts his case very clearly. He shows that McClellan was dividing his forces into two wings, which could not be brought together again in less than three or four weeks. Meanwhile the Confederates were left on interior lines and could concentrate against either wing ; this is the one great chance for which a commander with inferior numbers is always on the watch—McClellan made Johnston a present of it. But these arguments only condemn the water scheme without offering anything but mud as an alternative.

Henderson, without being enthusiastic over the water, prefers it to mud.

'The route from the coast, though little shorter, was certainly easier. Fort Monroe had remained in Federal hands. Landing under the shelter of its guns McClellan would push forward, aided by the navy, to West Point, the terminus of the York River Railroad, within thirty miles of Richmond, transporting his supplies by water. Washington, with the garrison he would leave behind, would in his opinion be quite secure. The Confederates would be compelled to concentrate for the defence of their Capital.' . . . 'Such was McClellan's reasoning, and, putting politics aside, it was perfectly sound.'

Looking at it through the spectacles of History we see that Ropes was right. McClellan failed to give the

Government an entire feeling of security; his information regarding numbers and geography was hopelessly wrong; and his opponents were brilliant men who seized every opportunity. But the council of generals had not the gift of prophecy; they took the plan as it was set before them by McClellan.

The Execution of the Plan. It is one thing, however, to prepare a plan on paper; it is another thing to carry it out. 'A bad plan well carried out is better than a good plan badly carried out.' Whatever may be thought of McClellan's scheme, there can be no doubt that it was ruined by thoroughly bad execution.

Here I assert without any hesitation that McClellan had only himself to blame. For eight months he had been in close touch with the President, and knew quite well that his scheme was only approved on the distinct understanding that Washington and Maryland should be safely guarded. We must give him credit for the belief that he had arranged it, but this was by no means sufficient. He was going off himself, leaving behind a President who had only given a reluctant consent; he was also aware that some of the Cabinet distrusted him; he had already begun to regard them as 'the enemies in his rear'. It was his duty to satisfy them, and apart from all duty it was only common sense to satisfy them before he went away.

It has been said that Lincoln ought to have demanded full details, and certainly his omission to do so points to a lack of business methods in his administration. But he trusted McClellan; once consent had been given to the scheme he left the execution in the hands of the soldiers, and did not want to cause friction or show distrust by pressing for details.

McClellan was so intent on the preparations for his expedition that he left the defence of Washington to the last moment. It was only when he was on board ship, about to start for Fort Monroe, that he sent in a detailed statement of the troops he proposed to leave behind. The numbers are shown on Table A, and demand careful scrutiny. They show gross and inexcusable carelessness.

TABLE A

McClellan's statement of numbers to be left for defence of Washington and Maryland

1. Total in Washington and forts . . 22,000
    Of these to be sent to Manassas . . 4,000

    Total left at Washington . . . 18,000   18,000

2. To be at Manassas
    The above 4,000 from Washington . . 4,000
    Troops now in Pennsylvania . . . 3,500
    Troops now guarding railways in Maryland 3,359

    10,859   10,859

3. To be at Warrenton
    Abercrombie's Division and Geary's force 7,780   7,780

4. To be in the Shenandoah Valley
    Blenker's Division 10,028
    Banks's Corps 19,687
    Cavalry 3,652
    Railroad guards 2,100

    . 35,467   35,467

5. Force on the Lower Potomac . . . 1,350

    Grand Total . . 73,456

Item 1. General Wadsworth, who commanded in Washington, reported on April 2nd that he had only 19,000 men fit for duty. If he sent 4,000 to Manassas there would be only 15,000 left. The corps commanders had recommended 35,000.

Item 2. McClellan had no right to count on men employed as railway guards, or on men whom he believed to be available in Pennsylvania. Therefore this force did not really exist at all.

Item 3. This force belonged to Banks's Corps, and McClellan counted it twice. It must either be struck out or subtracted from Item 4.

Item 4. Blenker's Division was under orders to join Fremont in Western Virginia, and McClellan was well aware of this. It ought not to have been counted as available for the defence.

Later on McClellan excused himself by arguing that the troops which he showed at Manassas and Warrenton (18,600) could fall back to Washington if the enemy advanced, and the garrison would then amount to 36,600.

Lincoln, however, could only take the numbers which were actually available—these amounted to 19,000 in Washington and 23,000 under Banks. He immediately referred McClellan's statement to General Thomas (Adjt.-General) and General Hitchcock (Military Adviser to the War Department). These two officers reported that 'the requirements of the President and the Corps Commanders had not been complied with'.

On this Lincoln would have been warranted in recalling McClellan for disobedience of orders. But the expedition had started. McClellan was undoubtedly popular with his men, and infinite trouble would have been caused by a drastic upset of the scheme.

Lincoln's Appreciation. McClellan was allowed to proceed with his army to the Peninsula. But, as he had failed to make satisfactory provision for the defence of Washington, Lincoln felt bound to take the responsibility on his own shoulders. As regards the numbers of the enemy he had no means of checking those given by McClellan. They might be correct—in which case the situation was serious, for Johnston could collect 115,000 for the invasion of Maryland. This would result (to quote Lee's expression) in 'swapping Queens', in other words Johnston could overrun the North while McClellan took the Capital of the South. Neither the country nor Lincoln could afford such an exchange.

Secondly, the numbers of the enemy might be exaggerated. Lincoln probably suspected that it might be so. But until this question could be settled more definitely he decided to adopt a middle course.

McDowell's Corps (32,500), which was being assembled at Alexandria for embarkation, was ordered to Fredericksburg. If the Confederates marched northwards he would be on their flank and rear. If they moved to the defence of Richmond the danger to Washington would be removed—McDowell could then move southwards and join hands with McClellan.

This was the first detention of McDowell. It was certainly justified by McClellan's disobedience. Whether it was wise from a military point of view will be discussed later on.

May '61. During the next seven weeks nothing of vital importance took place. Though Banks's force was gradually weakened to reinforce McDowell, he himself was confident that he could hold his own in 'the Valley'. McDowell, with 40,000 men, had pushed southwards a dozen miles from Fredericksburg and was expected to join hands with McClellan. The latter, working his way slowly from Fort Monroe, had established himself within sight of Richmond, and everything pointed to a decisive battle for the Capital of the Confederacy.

The Northern press once more heralded victory. A morning paper published a leader which was headed 'Fall of Richmond'. But on the same day as the people came out of church the newsboys were shouting 'Defeat of General Banks ! Washington in danger ! '

To understand the dramatic change in the situation we must turn to events in 'the Valley'.

VII

THE SHENANDOAH VALLEY

General Thomas J. Jackson.

HENDERSON has painted a vivid portrait of 'Stonewall', but it would please some of us better if the halo were not so much in evidence. History, as taught in the nursery, used to label our monarchs 'good' or 'bad'; some biographers of the last century, if more verbose, were almost equally sweeping in their judgements, and once a man was good he must be treated with proper reverence and awe. The present generation is more inquisitive, not altogether from lack of reverence, but from a desire for understanding and sympathy; a little human frailty brings the saint off his pedestal down to a plane where we can understand him better, and probably like him all the more.

Jackson was eighteen years of age when he entered the Military Academy at West Point in 1842. Tall and rather awkward in his movements, with a gravity beyond his years, he was noted as a conscientious but slow worker. He passed out seventeenth on the list—McClellan was first in the same class. Almost immediately he went through the campaign in Mexico as a subaltern of artillery.

After a couple of years of garrison life he accepted an appointment as Professor at the Virginian Military Institute at Lexington (100 miles west of Richmond). Here he spent ten uneventful years of routine, broken only by a trip to Europe. His lectures were learned but dull, and he was no favourite with the cadets. Though he did not shun society, there was nothing of the convivial companion about him.

An austere religion had become the governing factor in his life, and while there was no aggressive intolerance towards others, he allowed himself no latitude of any kind. He never smoked, drank, or touched a card. Observance of the Sabbath went so far that he would never open a letter on a Sunday ; ' he believed that the Government in carrying the mails on Sundays was violating a divine law, and that the suppression of such traffic was one of the most important duties of the Legislature '. In his correspondence we find ' a kindly Providence will enable us to inflict a terrible wound '— and the adjectives in this expression are characteristic.

To put it bluntly, he is a first-class prig—about as cheerful as Brother Stiggins, as humble as Uriah Heep— and we are prepared to dislike him thoroughly.

Rataplan ! Rataplan ! At the tap of the drum our sober prig vanishes, and in his place there appears a gambler, intoxicated with the red wine of war. His soaring imagination carries him to heights where without exaggeration he can be compared with Alexander, Charles XII of Sweden, Napoleon the Great. Each daring exploit seems more foolhardy than the last. A gallant fellow this—yet surely a bit reckless in his gambling ?

There is ' a little story ' of the niggers' poker party where the novice collected a hand of four aces ; this was good luck ; when he got them again it was very good luck ; but when he had held them five or six times it was adjudged to be good dealing.

If any one of Jackson's exploits be taken by itself he seems to have carried it through by sheer luck—but by the time we come to the end of the story we realize that there was no gambling at all ; every move was the result of shrewd calculation, based on a profound insight into the effect it would have on his immediate opponent and on the big situation. This is the real man at last—all former prejudices are swept away—we take back ' prig ' and ' gambler ' and write him down a genius of war.

It must, however, be admitted that his strategy is not free from the faults which seem inseparable from a 'one-man show '. Intent on deceiving and surprising his foe, he always kept his plans to himself and would not trust even his own staff or his brigade commanders. Until they got to know him they resented such treatment, and sometimes failed through bad co-operation. In the same way he was not a success as a subordinate, though there was no lack of confidence between him and Lee. His own brother-in-law, General D. H. Hill, said : ' Jackson's genius never shone when he was under the command of another. It seemed then to be shrouded or paralysed. MacGregor on his native heath was not more different from MacGregor in prison than was Jackson his own master from Jackson in a subordinate position. This was the keynote to his whole character. The hooded falcon cannot strike the quarry.'

In the Valley Jackson was given complete liberty ; his little force, which at no time exceeded 16,000, could be held under his own keen eye ; it had been drilled and marched till its extraordinary mobility made it a perfect machine for a perfect commander.

As early as October 1861 he had thought out the offensive operations at which the Confederates should aim.

' Crossing the upper Potomac, occupying Baltimore, and taking possession of Maryland, we could cut off the communications of Washington, force the Federal Government to abandon the Capital, beat McClellan's army if it came out against us in the open country, destroy industrial establishments wherever we found them, break up the mines, seize and if necessary destroy the manufactories and commerce of Philadelphia, and of other large cities within our reach ; subsist mainly on the country we traverse, and making unrelenting war amidst their homes, force the people of the North to understand what it will cost them to hold the South in the Union at the bayonet's point.'

It was well for the Union that Jackson was not free to carry out his plans. McClellan declared that the defence of Washington ' lay on the banks of the James River'. With the same idea, but with better execution, Jackson's defence of Richmond would have been somewhere north of the Potomac. The Southern President, however, would not permit aggressive action in 1861, and after that the Northern forces were too strong. Jackson, with reluctance, admitted that it was so, but this,did not mean there was nothing left for him to do—if he could not invade he could at least threaten to do it. With unerring judgement he saw that the nerve centre of the North lay in its commerce, the big industrial cities with their network of railways. Those cities, having sent their sons to the front, would demand, and had a right to demand, protection ; they were not sufficiently educated in the science of war to look upon an army in the Peninsula as a bulwark of Maryland.

Starting from this idea, the whole object of Jackson's famous campaign in the Valley was to ' play the bogey man '—in other words to send a message to the North that the Confederates in great force were about to cross the Potomac. The first thing was to give the enemy an exaggerated estimate of his numbers. 'Kindly Providence', though objecting to Sunday letters, would overlook deception when undertaken in a good cause. McClellan got his numbers from a firm of detectives, but I suggest that his chief source of information was *Jackson himself*. There is no direct evidence of this —there rarely can be direct evidence about espionage work. But Jackson was a student of Napoleon ; the great Corsican had paraded a dummy army, the sweepings of hospitals and garrisons, for the benefit of Austrian spies. A theatrical manager marches his army several times across the stage and round behind the scenes. McClellan's detectives, untrained in estimating numbers, might very well count them twice over. Whether it was due to Jackson's cunning or McClellan's credulity (or both) must be a matter of doubt, but the fact remains that the numbers of the Confederates which were reported as 115,000 were actually 53,000 ; of these Jackson was credited with 15,000 when he had less than 5,000.

Next, a bogey man must show no fear himself ; if you attack boldly the enemy will assume you have superior numbers ; Jackson acted on this principle, and though he refrained when he saw no hope of success he was ready to take considerable risks, feeling sure that even if the Federals repulsed him they would give him credit for greater numbers than he had.

Such was the intrepid leader who was lurking in the Valley, the ' back door to Washington '.

Lincoln, of course, knew nothing of Jackson, and had probably never heard of him before Bull Run. But he knew well the effect invasion would have on the North, and could not afford to ' swap Queens '. With the instinct of a strategist he saw the possibilities open to a clever enemy. ' Never take counsel of your fears ' is a high-sounding principle of war, but as Captain Cuttle says, ' the bearing of that there observation lies in the application of it.' A strong man has prudence, which is a virtue—a weak man has fear, which is the other thing.

With the fierce light of History thrown upon him the bogey of the Valley was nothing to be afraid of—he never had a force which could be a serious menace to Washington, and certain writers have got a lot of cheap fun out of this. Lincoln saw him not in the light of History but in the fog of war, and through the magnifying spectacles of McClellan's detectives—just an occasional glimpse, for he was as elusive as a will o' the wisp, with an occasional meeting, for the bogey could fight like a wild cat. Before passing judgement

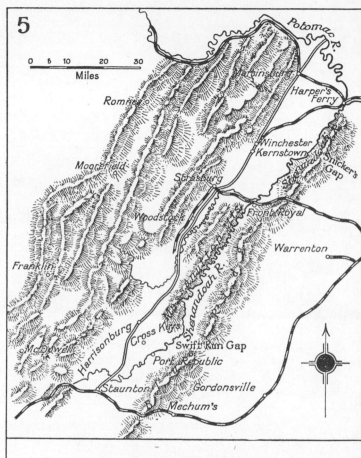

SHENANDOAH
VALLEY

let us resume the narrative, taking care to distinguish between the real facts and the reports that reached Washington.

Facts. In November 1861 Jackson was given command in the Valley, H. Q. at Winchester. Early in December he made a dash to the Potomac to damage the Chesapeake and Ohio canal, which runs along the north bank of the river. In January, having been joined by 6,000 men under Loring, he made a raid into Western Virginia, as far as Romney (forty miles west of Winchester). This was carried out in bitter weather. Jackson drove his troops over frozen roads, through icy rivers, with relentless discipline, which reduced Loring's men to a state of mutiny; in the end they had to be removed from his command, and he was left with 4,500.

Report to Washington. ' January. Jackson, strength unknown, very active. Wants watching.' On this General Banks, with 38,000, was ordered to advance towards Winchester and cover the rebuilding of the railway, which had been cut between Harper's Ferry and Martinsburg.

Facts. After Johnston's retreat from Manassas (March 9th) Jackson's position at Winchester was too exposed, and he fell back to Mount Jackson, forty miles up the Valley.

Report. ' Jackson has disappeared, leaving a strong cavalry screen behind him.' Banks occupied Winchester, March 12th. In accordance with McClellan's orders he now kept one division in the Valley (Shields) and sent one to Manassas (Williams).

Facts. Jackson had been trailing his coat southwards, hoping that Shields would tread on the tail of it. But Shields, after going a short way, was recalled to Winchester. Jackson had excellent information: the inhabitants were on his side to a man ; also he had a small but admirable force of cavalry under a born

leader, Colonel Ashby. On March 21st he heard
that Shields had retreated and that Federal Troops
were leaving the Valley. He immediately turned
northwards and marched thirty-six miles in two
days. At Kernstown, three miles south of Winchester, he came up with a force of Federals which
Ashby reported as being four regiments. The
Southerners were weary, they had marched fourteen
miles that day, it was already 4 p.m. (worst of all it
was a Sunday evening), but Jackson decided to
attack at once. His tactics were good (a strong
turning movement by the west), and his men fought
magnificently. But for once Ashby had made a
mistake and led Jackson into a trap—the whole of
Shield's division (7,000) lay behind the ridge. The
Confederates, completely outnumbered, were driven
back with considerable loss.

Report. 'March 24th. Jackson has reappeared. He
attacked Shields on the 23rd and was driven back.
Probably he is expecting reinforcements. Has disappeared again.' This looked as if the Confederates
meant mischief in the Valley. Lincoln ordered
Williams's division to go back from Manassas to
rejoin Banks. When McClellan had gone off to
Fort Monroe (April 1st) and it was found he had
left only 18,000 men in Washington, orders were
given to detain McDowell till the situation in the
Valley could be cleared up. This was the first
detention of McDowell.

Facts. Jackson retired leisurely up the Valley, and
went into camp at Swift Run Gap. There he remained, unmolested, till April 30th.

Report. 'Jackson is at Swift Run; all quiet.' As
Swift Run is over 100 miles from the Potomac,
Lincoln was now relieved of any immediate anxiety
about the Valley, and could turn his attention to the
Peninsular scheme. McDowell had already been

THOMAS JONATHAN ("Stonewall") JACKSON (1824–1863)
Lieutenant General, C.S.A.

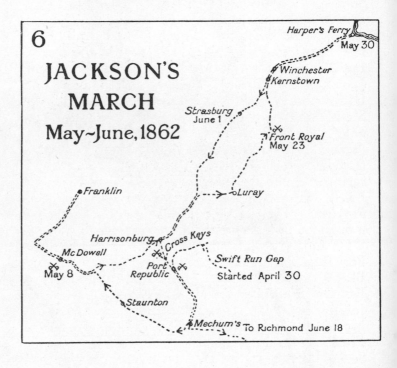

6

JACKSON'S
MARCH
May~June, 1862

Harper's Ferry
May 30

Winchester
Kernstown

Strasburg
June 1

Front Royal
May 23

Franklin

Luray

Harrisonburg
Cross Keys
McDowell
May 8
Port
Republic
Swift Run Gap
Started April 30

Staunton

Mechum's To Richmond June 18

moved to Fredericksburg; Banks was ordered to send Shields to join him there. This left Banks with only Williams's division (7,000). Fremont, who had 15,000 in Western Virginia, was ordered to cross the mountains in the direction of Staunton. Lincoln hoped that Fremont and Banks together would be able to deal with Jackson.

Facts. Jackson had 6,000 of his own. On April 29th two other forces were placed under him ; these were Ewell (8,000, close at hand) and Edward Johnson (3,000, near Staunton). He knew that Banks was at Harrisonburg, and that Fremont was moving on Staunton, strung out in three detachments. His object was to defeat the two opposing forces in detail. Banks was the nearer, but better concentrated. He decided first to reinforce E. Johnson and smash in Fremont's advanced guard, then to rejoin Ewell, turn upon Banks, and drive him over the Potomac. The best idea of his lightning campaign is obtained by a glance at the map (Sketch 6).

On April 30th Jackson left Swift Run, marched to Port Republic, then turned *eastward*, and crossed the Blue Ridge to Mechum's Station (all this to deceive Banks) ; thence by train to Staunton. Joined E. Johnson on May 5th and marched westward to McDowell Village (thirty miles). In camp here was Fremont's leading division (6,000) under Milroy. Seeing Jackson taking up a position on a high hill commanding the village and camp Milroy decided to attack. After four hours' fighting he was repulsed and made off northwards during the night, setting fire to the forests to obstruct pursuit. Jackson followed as far as Franklin, but finding that Fremont's whole force might be there he thought he had done enough in this direction and turned about to attack Banks.

Report. ' May 12th. Jackson has appeared again ;

fought Milroy at McDowell on May 8th and followed him to Franklin.' This made Jackson farther than ever from the Potomac ; but little hope was now left that Fremont could join Banks at the south end of the Valley ; so Banks was ordered to fall back to Strasburg and put a detachment at Front Royal.

Facts. Taking Ewell with him Jackson marched northward. He knew that Banks would expect him by the Valley turnpike which leads to Strasburg, so he made demonstrations in that direction ; then on May 21st he crossed the Massanutton Ridge by the single gap that exists in it ; on the 23rd he completely surprised the detachment at Front Royal and routed it. Having 16,000 against 7,000 he hoped to get behind Banks, cut him off from Winchester, and capture his whole force. In this, however, he failed. Banks made good his escape to Winchester ; then, having a secure line of retreat, he stood to fight just south of Winchester. He made a very good fight of it, but the Confederates were too strong, and he had to retire ; the battle had thrown his men into disorder, not very bad, but sufficient to make further resistance impossible, so he moved over the Potomac.

The reports about this were full and correct, as the facts. The situation now appeared to Lincoln as on Sketch 7. McDowell had been strengthened up to 40,000 ; he could be ordered either to push on to Richmond or to march to the Valley.

Lincoln decided to suspend McDowell's move on Richmond and send 20,000 of his men to march on Strasburg. He saw that Jackson (strength reported correctly at 16,000) was somewhere in the north end of the Valley, far from all support. Fremont was ordered from Franklin to Harrisonburg to stop the southern exit : Banks (reinforced to 16,000) was ordered to Winchester, to stop the northern exit : McDowell, marching on Strasburg, closed the eastern pass over the

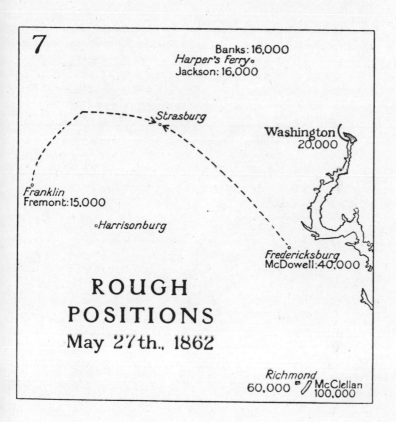

7

Banks: 16,000
Harper's Ferry○
Jackson: 16,000

Strasburg

Washington
20,000

Franklin
Fremont: 15,000

○Harrisonburg

Fredericksburg
McDowell: 40,000

ROUGH
POSITIONS
May 27th., 1862

Richmond
60,000 / McClellan
100,000

JEFFERSON DAVIS (1808–1889)
President of the Confederate States of America

Blue Ridge. Each of these three forces would be strong enough to fight Jackson or hold him till the other two came up. If they could converge on him with vigour they would crush him.

This was the second detention of McDowell. It must be strongly emphasized that Lincoln's plan was offensive. Some authors give the impression that it was defensive, caused by Lincoln's nervousness, the panic at Washington, and the bogey man at his best. This is entirely a mistake. It was true that there was excitement in the Capital, of which newspaper boys made the most. But the bogey no longer existed, or at least he had come out into the daylight and was revealed as Stonewall Jackson, numbers and location reported very correctly. Lincoln knew that Jackson could not cross the Potomac with so few men ; defensive action would only require a very small readjustment of his forces. He moved 60,000 men, not for defence but with a good hope of surrounding Jackson and crushing him. The attempt failed, but only by a few hours, and it might well have succeeded if the Federal commanders had played up to the intention of Lincoln.

Fremont thought the direct road from Franklin to Harrisonburg too bad (perhaps it was, Jackson had taken steps to obstruct it) ; he therefore made the long detour by Moorefield to Strasburg. Though his men had been resting at Franklin for ten days he took eight days to march seventy miles, and arrived at Strasburg on June 1st, just in time to see Jackson's rear-guard moving out of it to the southward.

McDowell's troops had about the same distance to go, seventy miles. The leading division (Shields's) reached Front Royal on May 30th—and halted. On June 1st McDowell pushed Shields to Strasburg—too late. Both Fremont and McDowell complained of the weather, but while they took eight days to march seventy miles, Jackson marched *fifty miles in two days*.

He had been at Harper's Ferry on the 30th when he heard of the forces directed against him ; he came to the conclusion that it was time to retire. On the 30th he reached Winchester, on the 31st Strasburg, and on June 1st he slipped away to the south, taking all his wagons with him.

Most of the critics condemn Lincoln's plan. The arguments appear to be, first that it failed, and second that McDowell would have been of more use elsewhere, that is, towards Richmond. With regard to the first, it is generally supposed that Lincoln was incapable of handling so delicate an operation as the convergence of three forces on one point. Colonel W. Allan, who was with Jackson, has written a very careful account of the Valley Campaign ; his book gives in detail the movements of each force and the orders issued by Lincoln. He shows very conclusively (pages 120–36) that the President understood the situation, and issued orders which would have led to success if they had been carried out with any thrust. Jackson's escape was due to his marvellous driving power, and to the hesitation not of Lincoln but of Fremont and Shields.

The second argument, that McDowell's force would have been of greater value elsewhere, is quite a separate question. It can only be discussed when the situation in the Peninsula is known. It is therefore relegated to Chapter IX.

June 1st–9th, Jackson retired southwards to Cross Keys. Fremont followed by the main road from Strasburg ; Shields moved on the parallel road in the Luray Valley ; they were separated by the Massanutton Ridge. Jackson decided to fight each of them in turn before they could join hands. On the 8th (Sunday) he halted to give battle to Fremont at Cross Keys. The Federals attacked hotly but were repulsed. Next day Jackson turned on the head of Shields's column : the engagement is known as the battle of Port Republic.

The Federals fought with skill and determination, but could not get up the rear to support the leading brigades, so were eventually driven back.

The campaign in the Valley was over. Jackson had not inflicted any decisive defeat on his opponents ; in fact, their total losses were under 4,000, while his amounted to 2,600. But he had certainly diverted McDowell's force from the Peninsula, which was his main object. He had also gained a reputation which was of infinite value to the South. Though always outnumbered in the theatre of the campaign he always had superior forces when he accepted battle, except on one occasion, Kernstown. His men, who had begun by groaning at his iron discipline, now carried out his very exacting demands with enthusiasm. He was a great leader.

Banks has come in for a good deal of ridicule which is unfair. He was operating in a hostile country, his cavalry was inferior to that of the Confederates, and consequently his information was bad. If Ashby, with a couple of hundred of his men who knew the Valley, could have been transferred to the other side, Banks would then have had the eyes which he needed—but as it was he was very blind. Consequently Jackson, who had the eyes, and also brains to make use of his information, beat Banks in manœuvre—but it took a Jackson to do it. Banks was always ready for a fight, and fought well.

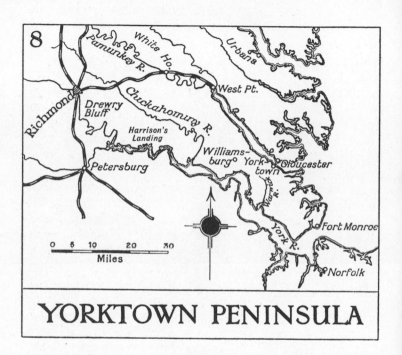

YORKTOWN PENINSULA

VIII

THE PENINSULA

McCLELLAN'S campaign began its unhappy course under the worst possible auspices. Even before the big question of the defence of Washington there were omens of trouble to come. Lincoln had frankly doubted the advisability of the scheme, and very properly asked questions about it ; but once he gave approval he was bent on making it a success. McClellan could not and would not understand this ; it seemed to him that questions about his plans only showed the ignorance and stupidity of the questioner ; the administration at Washington was the ' enemy in his rear ' ; even a consultation appeared to him like a reflection on his infallibility ; he avoided meeting Lincoln.

The Head of the State has the right to expect the full confidence of his subordinate, but as the subordinate showed every sign of objecting to consultations, the General in Chief of the Union issued some orders without consulting him.

In the first place he restricted McClellan to the command of the Army of the Potomac, which was destined for the Peninsula. The forces remaining in Virginia were divided into three departments : (1) Western Virginia, under Fremont, (2) the Shenandoah Valley under Banks, (3) from the Blue Ridge to the coast ; McDowell was later on appointed to this. It would be absurd to suppose that a general, face to face with the enemy in the Peninsula, could give proper attention to the whole theatre of war which extended through Virginia and Kentucky to the Mississippi, let

91

alone the training camps, arsenals, &c., all over the country. McClellan himself realized this. It has been accounted as virtue to him that ' he made no remonstrance '. It has been accounted as ' studied discourtesy ' on the part of the General in Chief that he did not consult his subordinate before issuing the order.

Lincoln never showed ' studied discourtesy ' to anybody in his life. But he did not shrink from making his meaning clear, and his meaning was that McClellan was not to interfere any further with matters outside the Peninsula and his own army of the Potomac.

Another step which has been much criticized was the removal of Blenker's Division from the Army of the Potomac to Fremont's department. There was some reason for this ; Lincoln was not the only man who looked upon the possession of Western Virginia as a matter of importance. The counties west of the mountains had broken away from the control of Richmond and declared for the Union. President Davis, Lee, Jackson were always thinking about this ; it was the one blot on the unanimity of the Confederacy, and thereby damaged the cause of the South in the eyes of the world. Jackson believed that the western counties were at heart loyal to the South and were only waiting to be relieved from the tyranny of Union bayonets. Lincoln read their minds and was determined not to lose hold. Besides this Fremont had a scheme for pushing down to Knoxville in Tennessee. The strategic importance of this railway junction was undeniable, and there were Unionists down there asking for succour. The idea was attractive, but Fremont was not the man to carry it out, nor was his force strong enough. He had more than enough to hold Western Virginia, not enough to do anything more. It cannot be denied that Blenker's Division was wasted. This is one of Lincoln's mistakes which I do not understand.

Another apparent mistake, much more mysterious, was the sudden closing of all recruiting. There must, of course, have been some reason, good or bad, but it has never come to light. From a military point of view it is absolutely unaccounted for.

Yorktown. The movement by sea was carried through without a hitch, which reflects much credit on those in charge of the arrangements. But after that obstacles cropped up which were far from creditable to the foresight of the commander. ' McClellan's fertile imagination only took into account his own operations. He seemed constitutionally incapable of allowing to his adversary sufficient sagacity to take even the most ordinary precautions.' [1]

The Confederate commander was General Magruder. At first he had only 13,000 men, and did not expect to repel the invaders, but with a view to gaining time he took the very obvious precaution of preparing a couple of positions across the Peninsula. The first had its left on Yorktown, and ran along the Warwick River ; this stream had been dammed in several places to make it unfordable ; field-works were thrown up to protect the dams. Yorktown had some remains of old fortifications which were extended and improved with new batteries. The length of the whole position was about thirteen miles.

McClellan had trusted to a map which turned out to be very incorrect. It showed the Warwick River running nearly parallel to the coast, and only two or three miles from it ; this left a gap between it and Yorktown of something like ten miles, and McClellan thought there would be no trouble in forcing it. The gap turned out to be less than two miles, and, in addition to field-works, was under the fire of the Yorktown guns. The Federals bumped into this unexpected obstacle.

[1] Wood and Edmonds, p. 55.

McClellan first asked for assistance from the navy to turn Yorktown by sea. Flag Officer Goldsborough was unable to give it ; the *Merrimac* was still in Norfolk and must be carefully blockaded ; the constant stream of vessels to and from Washington must be guarded ; in fact, his ships were fully employed. And, further, the channel at Yorktown was only 1,000 yards wide and was covered by batteries on the heights of Gloucester as well as those of Yorktown itself.

Next McClellan demanded reinforcements in order to take Gloucester. Lincoln eventually sent Franklin's Division (of McDowell's Corps), but it did not arrive till April 22nd, and even then no suitable place could be found for landing, so it never went ashore.

Meanwhile, McClellan had decided to reduce York-town by regular siege operations ; the work was carried on with much energy. On April 16th General W. F. Smith made a bold reconnaissance and actually suc-ceeded in crossing the river, but he was unsupported and had to fall back again. Parallels were opened, batteries erected, and heavy guns emplaced. All was ready for the bombardment to begin on May 6th when the Con-federates evacuated the whole position and retired.

It must remain a matter of argument whether it would have been possible to break the defence by assault. Ropes says : ' It was probably possible during the first half of April to break the Confederate lines at some point.' On the 14th General J. E. Johnston arrived with reinforcements and took over command from Magruder. He wrote to Lee : ' No one but McClellan could hesitate to attack.' On the other hand, the Federal engineer officers reported, after careful recon-naissance, that an assault would be very costly ; McClellan saw no use in losing lives to gain a position which could be forced by bombardment.

However that may be, it is easy to imagine the im-pression left on Lincoln's mind by this unforeseen check.

The whole scheme had been based on McClellan's optimistic assertion that it would go with a rush. At the end of a month the Federals had scarcely advanced twenty miles. Optimism had given place to complaints about the navy and the delay of reinforcements ; the landing-place at Fort Monroe was bad, the weather was bad, the roads were bad, the Warwick River ran the wrong way, and at Gloucester there was no landing place at all. Worse than this, as early as April 7th McClellan telegraphed : ' It seems clear that I shall have the whole force of the enemy on my hands, probably not less than 100,000, possibly more.'

McClellan had nobody but himself to blame if these reports were taken seriously. They proved that his information and calculations had been hopelessly wrong, and naturally this raised a feeling of distrust at Washington. And naturally, too, Lincoln felt more strongly than ever that he must take on his own shoulders the defence of the Potomac. He was willing to give McClellan all the help he could, but he would not run risks for the sake of a success which seemed daily to be farther and farther away. Keeping in mind this impression, which kept on growing, we can deal briefly with the narrative.

May–June, 1862. The Confederates had retired, and the Federals, following them, bumped into the second obstacle ; this was a line of detached redoubts near Williamsburg. This had been so little expected that when the collision occurred McClellan himself was ten miles back at Yorktown ; there he was superintending the re-embarkation of Franklin's Division, which was now to go up the York River to West Point. Consequently the battle of Williamsburg was undertaken by the generals who happened to be on the spot, and, as might be expected, there was no definite plan about it. The Federals blocked each other at one point and left gaps at others ; they attacked gallantly but could not break the line. The Confederates, however, did not intend to make any prolonged stand, and during the night they resumed their leisurely way to Richmond.

At the same time Norfolk was abandoned by the Southerners, and as the *Merrimac* was unable to ascend the James River she was blown up by her own commander. This gave the North undisputed command of the James River as far as Drewry's Bluff, seven miles from Richmond.

By May 21st McClellan had established himself within twelve miles of his goal, with his base at White House. Two Corps were sent across the Chickahominy, but as McDowell was now expected from Fredericksburg three Corps were left on the north bank to join hands with him. The result was that the army was divided into two wings by the river—a muddy unfordable stream, very liable to floods. McClellan fully realized the danger of such a position, astride a river, and he worked hard to get a number of bridges thrown across.

Such was the situation on May 25th when the news was received that McDowell had been detained for the second time, in order to chase Jackson. The Army of the Potomac had been nearly two months in the Peninsula ; it had advanced sixty miles ; the only battle that had been fought (Williamsburg) was an unpremeditated *affaire de rencontre*.

It is generally considered that on receiving the news about McDowell it would have been better for McClellan to concentrate his whole force on the south bank of the Chickahominy, and transfer his base from White House to the James River. He thought of this, but deferred doing it probably in hopes that McDowell might be sent to him later on.

Before the bridges were completed Johnston took advantage of the false position of the Federals ; he attacked the two corps on the south bank, confident that they could not be reinforced. This resulted in the battle of Fair Oaks (or Seven Pines), May 31st and June 1st.

On the first day the Federals were pushed back about a mile and a half. Sumner's Corps managed to get across from the north bank during the afternoon, and with his help the battle was restored ; the Federals now took the offensive and the enemy was forced back to his original line.

After this there was a pause for over three weeks. Both sides were busy entrenching. McClellan telegraphed : ' I shall be in perfect readiness to move forward and take Richmond the moment McCall reaches here and the ground will admit the passage of artillery.' McCall's Division belonged to McDowell's Corps, and Lincoln had promised to send it by sea. It arrived at the front on June 12th, and the weather became very favourable on June 14th. Yet another fortnight went by in preparations. McClellan states that everything was ready for his attack on June 26th. But it was the Confederates who attacked and a dramatic change took place.

General R. E. Lee. Johnston had been severely wounded in the battle of Fair Oaks, and was succeeded by the great commander who, from this date, controlled all the Southern forces in Virginia.

General Lee had been universally recognized as the best soldier in the war. Sir F. Maurice, in a book recently published, places him very high among the great commanders of History.

From the first Lee had a fine grip of the situation. He was able to locate the enemy's forces, almost to a man ; his own forces were on interior lines ; he understood the general who was opposed to him. Henderson says : ' Lee read McClellan like an open book.' For the moment Jackson's exploits in the Valley had kept back the reinforcements which McClellan was known to be expecting. It was therefore time to strike a blow before these reinforcements could arrive. Taking advantage of his interior lines Lee could concentrate to strike either at McClellan or at Washington. The latter course would probably result in ' swapping Queens ', and it is possible that it would have been more effective. If, however, the Army of the Potomac could be driven into the sea, the invasion of the North could be undertaken afterwards, with all the more prospect of success, and without the risk of sacrificing Richmond. This decided Lee to call in Jackson from the Valley and attack McClellan.

The Seven Days. On June 25th the Army of the Potomac had four Corps on the south of the Chickahominy River ; they were strongly entrenched and faced the entrenchments of the Confederates, about four miles east of Richmond. On the north bank lay a single Corps—Porter's. The base was at White House, whence supplies were sent up by railway ; a glance at the map shows that the railroad runs for twenty-five miles on the north bank of the river. Though several bridges had been built to connect the two banks, the position was tactically unsound.

Lee decided to concentrate and attack Porter's Corps on the north bank ; this would cut McClellan off from his base.

Magruder was left with 27,000 Confederates on the south bank to face 67,000 Federals ; Lee took the rest of his troops to the north bank ; Jackson was to come in still farther north ; this would make an offensive mass of 53,000 to attack Porter's 23,000.

There was, of course, a risk that McClellan would attack on the south bank ; but even if he suspected that the line in front of him had been thinned out he would

GEORGE BRINTON MCCLELLAN (1826–1885)
Major General, U.S.A.

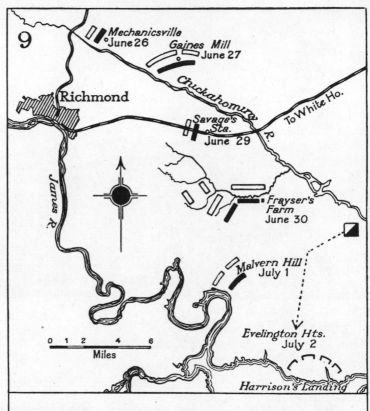

THE SEVEN DAYS

June 26th.~July 2nd., 1862

probably reconnoitre and waste time ; then the threat at his communications would divert his attention. In fact, with McClellan in command, the risk was small.

First Day, June 26th, Mechanicsville. Jackson was due to reach the extreme north of Porter's line at 8 a.m. He himself had fixed the hour, but owing to bad maps and bad guides he was not up to time. A. P. Hill, commander of the Confederates who came from the south bank, did not wait for Jackson's turning movement but attacked by himself and was repulsed ; it was a serious failure in co-operation. The Federal force at Mechanicsville was the Division of McCall (attached to Porter), and during the night it was drawn in to join the main body of the Corps.

Second Day. June 27th, Gaines' Mill, or Cold Harbor. Porter was in a strong semicircular position. Once more Lee sent Jackson to make a flanking movement by the north ; once more Jackson was late. During the first two hours of the battle Porter's men, fighting gallantly, held their own ; but when Jackson's attack developed on their right they were overpowered by numbers. McClellan sent two brigades from the south bank to cover the retreat, which was carried out in surprisingly good order. The Northerners had lost their position, but their casualties (about 7,000) were less than those of the South (8,000).

McClellan saw that he was cut off from White House, and immediately ordered his ships to move round and establish a new base at Harrison Landing on the James River. Though it was necessary to abandon some stores the movement was carried out with much skill, and it is generally recognized that it saved the situation. ' McClellan showed himself at his best in conducting this retreat. He was above everything else an organizer, and organization rather than generalship was what was needed just then.'[1]

Third Day, June 28th. Lee believed that McClellan would retreat to Fort Monroe, which meant that the Federals would have to recross the Chickahominy. Stuart's cavalry was pushed along the north bank to look out for them. The Federals, however, were busy getting their wagons across White Oak Swamp and were making due south.

Fourth Day, June 29th, Savage Station. Lee ordered Jackson to cross the Chickahominy, and Magruder to leave his entrenched lines ; the two were to make a combined attack. But Jackson took the whole day to repair the bridges which the Federals had demolished. Only a rearguard action took place in the evening near Savage Station.

Fifth Day, June 30th, Glendale, or Frayser's Farm. McClellan took up a position with his front facing north on White Oak Swamp, and his left thrown back to guard against a flank attack from the direction of Richmond. Lee's intention was to send a turning movement well to the south, but again the Confederates missed an opportunity by bad co-operation. Jackson could not find his way across the swamp. Of the other columns, Longstreet's was the only one to make a resolute assault, and though he got into the Federal line and took some guns, he was forced out again.

It is an extraordinary fact that though the Southerners were within ten miles of their own capital they had no maps which showed the roads and paths correctly. The Federals, on the other hand, had excellent maps ; General Averell, a cavalry commander, had employed his officers during the month's halt in making sketches of all the ground ; these were of infinite value

---

[1] Wood and Edmonds, p. 73.

in helping the Federals to get their baggage away. It is very possible that if the Confederates had been in possession of those maps their co-operation would not have failed.

Sixth Day, July 1st, Malvern Hill. During the night McClellan had moved back steadily. The position he occupied at Malvern Hill was wisely selected; it ran along the crest from which the ground sloped down like a glacis to the woods and swamps at the bottom; the flanks were protected by marshy streams; the gunboats on the James River could bring fire to bear on the west side of the field. The Confederates were scarcely able to bring artillery into action at all.

Lee ordered an attack, under the impression that the Army of the Potomac was demoralized. In this he was mistaken; the Federals were well in hand and admirably posted—they showed no unsteadiness. The Confederate attack never had a chance and was repulsed with heavy slaughter.

Seventh Day, July 2nd. In spite of the real success at Malvern Hill, McClellan decided to continue his retreat on Harrison Landing. Stuart's Cavalry, which since Gaines' Mill had been scouring along the Chickahominy, appeared on Evelington's Heights, a hill overlooking the Federal camp. But Stuart could not maintain his position with cavalry alone, and had to move away.

This ended the fighting in the Peninsula. The Federal casualties during the Seven Days were 16,000, including 6,000 prisoners; they also lost 52 guns and 35,000 rifles. The Confederate casualties were higher, about 20,000; as they had been the attackers all the time this was not unnatural—but, with their dwindling numbers, they could ill afford the loss.

On the fields of battle honours were fairly divided; the Federal defeat at Gaines' Mill was balanced by the victory at Malvern Hill, and the other fighting had been indecisive. Lee was bitterly disappointed at his failure to destroy the Federals completely. All the same he had gained a moral success ; the invading army which had sat for over a month within sight of Richmond had been driven back sixteen miles and was in no condition to renew its advance.

McClellan entrenched his position at Harrison Landing and sat still. Lee withdrew his troops to Richmond.

IX

LINCOLN AND McCLELLAN

IT is now possible to revert to Lincoln's attitude, which has been so severely condemned. As stated in Chapter VI, McClellan's carelessness and disobedience in arranging the garrison of Washington was sufficient to justify the detention of McDowell's Corps. The question remains whether it ruined the campaign.

To my mind the answer is to be found in McClellan's own book—a full and complete answer. It is not pleasant reading, and adds little or nothing to our knowledge of historical facts; indeed, it has been almost ignored by most writers. Ropes dismisses it curtly—'McClellan has written a book in which he acquits himself of everything except egoism'. But it is a very human document, a true revelation of the character of the man, and if we wish to get inside Lincoln's mind and see his train of thought, it gives us a direct clue that is worth following.

McClellan's Own Story. 'July 27th. I find myself in a new and strange position here (Washington)—President, Cabinet, Gen. Scott, and all deferring to me. By some strange operation of magic I seem to have become the power of the land.' ... 'I went to the Senate and was quite overwhelmed by the congratulations I received and the respect with which I was treated.' ... 'They give me my way in everything, full swing and unbounded confidence.'

For the moment everything is the colour of roses, but unfortunately roses soon fade. Trouble began with General Scott over minor questions of organization, in which the Young Napoleon was probably quite right; but the rather testy old gentleman did not relish being patronized and corrected by one who might almost have been his grandson.

August 5th. 'Gen. Scott is, the great obstacle. He will not comprehend the danger. I have to fight my way against him.' August 16th. 'I am here in a terrible place : the enemy have three to four times my force ; the President, the old general, cannot and will not see the true state of affairs.' October 6th. 'My plans depend upon circumstances. So soon as I feel that my army is well organized and well disciplined, and strong enough, I will advance and force the rebels to a battle in a field of my own selection.'

' My relations with Mr. Lincoln were generally very pleasant, and I seldom had trouble with him when we could meet face to face. I believe that he liked me personally, and certainly he was always much influenced by me when we were together. During the early part of my command in Washington he often consulted with me before taking important steps or appointing general officers.'

In the course of October the country began to murmur about an advance, and McClellan argues at much length that it was impossible. Lincoln suggested a raid on the Confederate batteries which were blocking the mouth of the Potomac.

' I did not regard the inconvenience resulting from the presence of the enemy's batteries on the Potomac as sufficiently great to justify the direct efforts necessary to dislodge them.'

Then came the illness in December. The President apparently had no business to consult other generals at this time—everything ought to have waited for McClellan's recovery. In February he proposed the movement by sea.

' The fears of the administration and their inability to comprehend the merits of the scheme, or else the determination that I should not succeed in the approaching campaign, induced them to prohibit me from carrying out the Urbana movement. They gave me the choice between the direct overland route, via Manassas, and the route with Fort Monroe as a base. Of course I selected the latter.'

'Of course.' The whole book might almost be summed up in these two words. Once an idea took his fancy it was 'of course'. It mattered nothing that in August he himself had proposed the Manassas route, or that he had very little information about the Peninsula. Of course, his scheme was right. Those who did not agree with him were full of fear, or 'geese', or traitors to their country.

Here a pause may be made to note that it is not unusual to find a general complaining about the Government. Plenty of similar cases can be quoted from history. The general always wants just a little more—more men, more munitions, more supplies, while the Government, responsible to the country for finance, has to keep a watchful and sometimes a suspicious eye on expenditure. Wellington was often at loggerheads with the Cabinet, but, bitterly as he complained, he never accused a fellow countryman of a deliberate intention to ruin his campaign.

April 1st. On the steamer to Fort Monroe. 'I did not feel safe till I could fairly see Alexandria behind us. If I remained there I would be annoyed very much and perhaps be sent for from Washington.'

Then comes the arrival in the Peninsula and his scheme is fairly started.

April 3rd. 'I hope to get possession of Yorktown day after to-morrow. I see my way very clearly, and, with my trains once ready, will move rapidly.'

April 5th. 'I feel sure of to-morrow. I have, I think, provided against every contingency, and shall have the men well in hand if we fight to-morrow.'

April 6th. 'Things quiet to-day; very little firing.'

'I received an order detaching McDowell's Corps from my command. It is the most infamous thing that history has recorded.'

April 8th. 'I have raised an awful row about McDowell's Corps. The President very coolly telegraphed me yesterday that he thought I had better break the enemy's lines at once.

I was much tempted to reply that he had better come and do it himself.'

April 11th. 'I am sure that I will win in the end in spite of all their rascality. History will present a sad record of these traitors who are willing to sacrifice the country and its army for personal spite and personal aims.'

May 14th. A dispatch to the President. 'I cannot bring into actual battle against the enemy more than 80,000 men at the utmost, and with them I must attack in position, probably entrenched, a much larger force, perhaps double my numbers.'

Note the date of this, May 14th. This was how McClellan envisaged his prospects ; ten days later the President had to decide whether to send McDowell to chase Jackson or to send him to reinforce McClellan for an attack on double his numbers in a strong entrenched position.

May 17th. 'I am now at this present moment involved in a great many different orders for parties to move out at day-break on reconnaissances.' (Nothing happened on May 18th.)

'During the day and night of May 30th a very violent storm occurred. . . . The enemy seeing the unfavourable position in which we were placed threw an overwhelming force upon the position occupied by Casey's Division.'

This refers to the battle of Fair Oaks. It is interesting to note that the rains which had constantly made the roads impassable for McClellan were seized by the enemy as a good opportunity for attacking. As Lincoln once said : ' McClellan thinks that Heaven always sends rain on the just and never on the unjust.'

June 7th. 'I shall be in perfect readiness to move forward and take Richmond the moment McCall reaches here and the ground will admit the passage of artillery.'

June 13th. 'On the 12th and 13th Gen. McCall's Division arrived.'

June 14th. 'All quiet in every direction. Weather now very favourable.'

June 25th. 'I incline to think that Jackson will attack my right and rear. The rebel force is stated at 200,000. But if the result of the action, which will probably occur to-morrow or within a short time, is a disaster, the responsibility cannot be thrown on my shoulders ; it must rest where it belongs.'

For once McClellan was right in foretelling an action to-morrow. It was the beginning of the Seven Days.

' On the 26th, the day upon which I had decided as the time for our final advance, the enemy attacked our right in strong force, and turned my attention to the protection of our communications and depots of supply.'

There are over six hundred pages, very much to the same effect, with some account of the enthusiasm of the army whenever ' little Mac ' appeared upon the scene.

The extracts are from dispatches and private letters written at the time, but the book was compiled by McClellan about twenty years later, and he apparently saw nothing that needed explanation or correction. We see a careful and energetic organizer ; perhaps no man could be found better able to train an army and lead it to the bank of the Rubicon. But there he came to a dead stop.

He has been accused of hesitation, over-caution, timidity, but none of these words really fits. Hesitation is certainly wrong ; McClellan never hesitated about anything in his life ; it is quite a mistake to picture him trembling on the brink and trying to screw up courage for the plunge. Not a bit of it. The river was impassable—of course, it was—and nobody but a fool would attempt it till to-morrow. Timidity is not the right term ; he was physically brave ; his assurance is shown by the calm way in which he pursued his own path regardless of suggestions, appeals, or even definite orders ; his letters to the Government contain terms which are far from timid, and might be called impertinent. There certainly was caution, plenty of it, but even this word is not satisfying, because from his point of view the caution was quite justifiable. Perhaps we can get nearest to it by saying that his organizing faculties were overdeveloped, and he was governed by an overwhelming desire to complete his preparations. His victory must be certain and complete.

His words are worth repeating : ' So soon as I feel that my army is well organized and well disciplined, and strong enough, I will advance.' Needless to say all generals who ever commanded armies have longed for such ideal conditions. But they have been wise enough to see that in this uncertain world war is of all things the most uncertain, and therefore it is useless to wait for a certainty ; besides which, while you wait, the enemy may be doing something.

Numbers. ' So soon as I feel that my army is strong enough.' This brings us to the matter of numbers. In Table B will be found his estimates, of his own forces as well as of the Confederates. In the other column are given the actual figures, extracted from the Official Records, which were very carefully compiled and may be taken as correct. But to get the *effective* strength of the Federals we ought to subtract about one-fifth of the gross numbers, for their states included servants, grooms, and various non-effectives.

TABLE B.   *Forces in the Peninsula.*

Date	McClellan's Estimate		Actual Numbers
April 7th	South	' 100,000 possibly more '	13,000 reinforced to 53,000
,,	North	' 40,000 for attack '	108,000
May 14th	South	' Probably double my numbers '	53,000
,,	North	80,000	128,000
June 25th	South	200,000	86,000
,,	North	about 90,000	128,000

Looking at the actual figures we see that an addition of 35,000 (McDowell's Corps) would give the Federals a very fine superiority of numbers over the Confederates. Lord Wolseley is quite right in saying that McDowell's

35,000 would have put McClellan in a position to gain
a decisive victory.   But the whole question is whether
McClellan would have used them.   To answer this
reference must be made to McClellan's own estimate ;
an addition of 35,000 on any date does not bring
him up to the enemy's strength.   ' So soon as *I* feel
that my army is strong enough I will attack.'   This
answers the question quite clearly—McClellan would
not have attacked.   If any one doubts this let him study
McClellan's book ; I have read it several times (not for
pleasure) and each time confirms my conviction that
McClellan would not have attacked.

The Strategist.   Starting from the premise that
McClellan would not attack, it is only a short step to
the next argument.   *Lincoln knew that McClellan would
not attack.*

Lord Charnwood says that Lincoln had not the gift
of rapid perception, but ' when he had known a man
long or been with him or against him in important
transactions, he sometimes developed great insight and
sureness of touch'.   For eight months he had been
studying McClellan, and by going over the ground once
again I believe we can get an idea of the thoughts in
the mind of the Strategist.

We see the President after Bull Run, resolute, un-
flinching, but sadly at a loss in the search for a commander of his forces.   To him enters the young general,
brimming over with ideas and energy.   Order is evolved
out of chaos, troops are disciplined, forts spring up,
and Washington is made secure.   Easy to imagine how
Lincoln's heart warmed as he saw the progress that was
made.

Then just a little cloud—the Confederate batteries
on the Potomac.   It appeared that these were trifles,
which must await the good pleasure of the general
who was busy with big things.

When the general fell ill in December the President was refused admission to his bedside, though the general admits he was doing business with his own staff. There was no certainty when he would recover ; he might not recover at all. The President thought he had a right to seek counsel from other officers. McDowell was one of these, and he has left a record of the consultations ; Lincoln was terribly despondent, his words were : ' If something was not done soon the bottom would be out of the whole affair.'

Ropes is very contemptuous about this despondency. ' The army near Washington was large and constantly increasing; it was in excellent spirits and fine condition.' . . . ' There was, in reality, nothing to cause despondency in the mind of any man at all accustomed to affairs on a large scale.' But here I venture to disagree with even so eminent an author. It was just the excellence of the army that made the President long for a man who would use it. When no plan for action could be found the President, sorely puzzled, had every reason to be despondent.

On January 12th McClellan ' mustered strength enough to be driven to the White House, where my unexpected appearance caused very much the effect of a shell in a powder magazine '. His account of the Cabinet Meeting which followed is worth all the money that any one pays for his book. Chase said the Cabinet wanted to know McClellan's plans—' the uncalled-for violence of his manner surprised me, but I determined to avail myself of it by keeping perfectly cool.' The President calmed down the uncalled-for violence, and McClellan scored off everybody.

On January 22nd was issued the ' President's General War Order No. 1 ' : ' That the 22nd day of February 1862, be the day for a general movement of the land and naval forces of the United States against the insurgent forces.' This order has been condemned as ' a curious

specimen of puerile impatience'. In ordinary circumstances it would be so, but the circumstances were
not ordinary; the Head of the State had exhausted
every means of persuasion and argument (I think he
had lost his temper, and I hope so); nothing was left
but to force a decision by order, and the drastic terms
in which it was couched were intended to shake
McClellan out of his serenity. It succeeded in ex-
tracting a proposal for action—a movement by sea.

Lincoln hesitated. He could understand the argument that an attack on Richmond would draw the
Confederates away from Washington, but instinct already whispered that McClellan would not attack. On
the other hand, the senior officers told him that the
Peninsular Scheme offered the only hope of early success. Conscious of his own ignorance of the science of
war, he accepted their decision.

Then came McClellan's statement of the troops to
be left behind. Lincoln must have kicked himself
(he deserved it) for neglecting to go into details before
McClellan sailed. But there was no more hesitation;
he was responsible to the country for the safety of
Washington, and that must be his first consideration.
There was, however, a possibility that McClellan
would act when he found himself face to face with the
enemy, so Lincoln set himself patiently to make the
best of things. On April 9th he wrote a long letter:

'MY DEAR SIR,—Your despatches complaining that you are
not properly sustained, while they do not offend me, do pain me
very much. . . . After you left I ascertained that less than 20,000
unorganized men, without a single field battery, were all
you designed to be left for the defence of Washington and
Manassas. . . . My implicit order that Washington should, by the
judgment of all the commanders of army corps, be left entirely
secure, had been neglected. It was precisely this that drove me
to detain McDowell. . . . And allow me to ask you, Do you
really think I should permit the line from Richmond via Manassas
Junction to this city to be entirely open except what resistance

could be presented by less than 20,000 unorganized troops ? ...
I suppose the whole force which has gone forward for you is
with you by this time. And if so I think it is the precise time
for you to strike a blow. By delay the enemy will relatively
gain on you—that is he will gain faster by fortifications and
reinforcements than you will by reinforcements alone. And
once more let me tell you that it is indispensable to you that
you strike a blow. I am powerless to help this. You will do me
the justice to remember I always insisted that going down the
bay in search of a field, instead of fighting at or near Manassas,
was only shifting and not surmounting a difficulty ; that we
should find the same enemy, and the same or equal entrenchments at either place. The country will not fail to note, is now
noting, that the present hesitation to move upon an entrenched
enemy is but the story of Manassas repeated. I beg to assure
you that I have never written you or spoken to you in greater
kindness of feeling than now, nor with a fuller purpose to sustain
you, so far as in my judgment I consistently can. But you must
act.'

The unexperienced lawyer summed up in three lines
the situation which the professional soldier was constitutionally incapable of realizing. ' By delay the
enemy will relatively gain on you—that is he will gain
faster by fortifications and reinforcements than you will
by reinforcements alone.'

The reply of the professional soldier to this was that
though the official states showed he had over 100,000
men, ' I had—after deducting guards and working
parties—much less than 40,000 for attack.'

By the middle of May McDowell had been reinforced
up to 40,000 and was moving from Fredericksburg.
Then came the news that Jackson was driving Banks to
the Potomac, and the great question arose, should
McDowell be sent to Richmond or to the Valley ?

' In war men are nothing ; it is the Man who is
everything.' This was one of those exaggerations in
which Napoleon delighted, to emphasize the value of
genius as compared with mere numbers. Nearly every
military writer has quoted it when talking of the

brilliance of Lee and Jackson. But in the case of
Lincoln some of them have fallen into the pit that they
have digged for others. They do a little sum in arithmetic to prove that McClellan would have taken
Richmond ; therefore Lincoln was wrong—an interfering politician.

Lincoln could do simple arithmetic. Had he not, as
a child, done sums on a spade with a lump of chalk ?
After adding up the numbers he looked beyond them
at the Man. If he had seen a Grant, a Sheridan, a
Sherman, there would have been no hesitation and
McDowell would have marched southwards at once.
But all he saw was McClellan, sitting in eternal rain,
and facing a strong position held by 200,000 of the
enemy. Was Lincoln wrong ?

'*In war men are nothing ; it is the Man who is everything.*' Let me underline those words before asserting
that Lincoln was not only justified, but more than that
—he provides a perfect example of a true appreciation
of Napoleon's maxim.

X

SECOND BULL RUN

McCLELLAN took some credit to himself for 'saving the army', but these three words are sufficient to show that the Peninsular Scheme had failed. Its object had been to take Richmond, purely offensive; during the Seven Days McClellan had fought on the defensive, and, however much credit was due to him and his gallant men for the fighting, the fact remained that he ended up sixteen miles farther away from his goal.

His spirits soon recovered. His own view was that the ' defence of Washington lay on the banks of the James ' : heavy reinforcements should be sent him at once ; there was still a possibility of taking Richmond, in fact, even on June 28th he wrote : ' Had I 20,000 or even 10,000 fresh troops to use tomorrow, I could take Richmond ' : at all events he could prevent the Confederates from taking their troops away for use elsewhere.

There was something to be said in favour of this. Indeed, if the actual figures are taken there is much to be said. The Confederates had 65,000 left. The Army of the Potomac had 90,000 ; and there were 20,000 reinforcements available. But as usual McClellan spoilt the sum by persistent iteration that the Confederates had 200,000. Lincoln, no doubt, saw that such figures could not be true, but also saw that while McClellan believed in them he would not attack. From the military point of view it was necessary to come to an immediate decision, and there were two courses open.

First : Withdraw all troops from the Peninsula back

to the Washington front. This was the safer plan. But it gave up hope of immediate offensive action ; it would be an open confession of failure.

Second : Keep on with the Peninsular Scheme on the principle that attack is the best form of defence ; risk invasion of the North ; send every available man to Harrison Landing ; replace McClellan himself by a thruster who would keep on hitting. But the risk was great against an opponent like Lee ; if he saw that the Federals could not be kept out of Richmond he might play the big game of swapping Queens.

Lincoln took neither one course nor the other and from the military point of view he certainly laid himself open to charges of indecision and hesitation. But this was a crisis in which the Strategist had to take counsel of the Statesman. The hopes of the North had been raised very high when the press announced that the fine Army of the Potomac was actually within sight of Richmond ; those hopes had been damped by the Seven Days ; a withdrawal would extinguish them altogether. Nothing would be left but the dreary prospect of beginning all over again. At such a moment even the stout hearts of the North might be tempted by the specious arguments of the peacemaker.

My belief is that he never lost grip, there was no indecision ; he decided from the first to withdraw from the Peninsula, but in order to give time for the disappointment to wear off he deferred the movement. The force at Harrison Landing was in a very strong position, its communications perfectly secure, and McClellan was quite competent as long as no offensive action was required. If the Confederates went on attacking so much the better. If, on the other hand, they turned northwards to attempt invasion, there were 50,000 Federals to oppose them ; the threat would rouse the fighting spirit of the North. The order for the withdrawal was not issued until August 3rd.

July 1862. General Halleck had been appointed Commander-in-Chief, under the President, and took up his duties on July 22nd. He was a regular soldier and had won a reputation in the West. The appointment was not a success and he has been very much criticized. There is, however, no evidence that his advice had any weight either for good or evil in the big questions, so it is not necessary to discuss his work, which dealt chiefly with matters of routine. He began with an attempt to get on friendly terms with McClellan, but when he did not yield to the unceasing demands for reinforcements he was classed with ' the rest of the gang ' ; the correspondence degenerated into peevish recriminations which, fortunately, need not be quoted. We can turn attention to the centre of gravity which was shifting northwards.

General Pope. After the failure of the attempt to catch Jackson at the end of May, Lincoln decided to appoint one commander for all the forces covering the Potomac. His choice fell on General Pope who, like Halleck, had been serving in the West. There were now under his command the three Corps of Banks, Sigel (*vice* Fremont), and McDowell, amounting to 50,000 in all. He started badly by issuing a bombastic proclamation to his army, which insinuated that the forces in Virginia were inferior to those of the West, where they were accustomed to see the backs of the enemy. But, apart from this, his first actions, which were vigorous, have generally won approval. The instructions given him were to guard Washington, secure the Valley, and create a diversion for the benefit of McClellan's army. He proposed to concentrate his three Corps at Warrenton and move on Gordonsville. Banks's Corps led the way.

Meanwhile Lee had come to the conclusion that there was nothing more to be feared from McClellan.

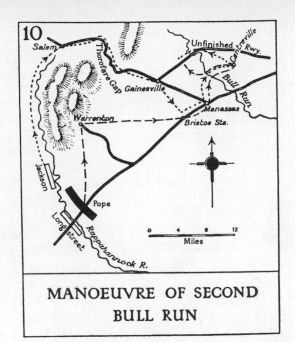

MANOEUVRE OF SECOND
BULL RUN

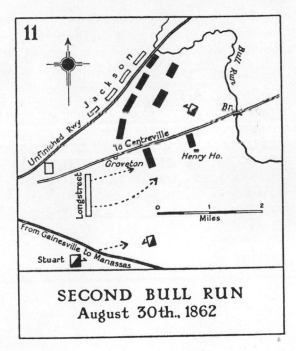

SECOND BULL RUN
August 30th., 1862

JOHN POPE (1822–1892)
Major General, U.S.A.

As early as July 13th Jackson had been sent with two
Divisions to Gordonsville ; towards the end of the
month he was joined by A. P. Hill, and his force
amounted to 24,000. With these he was advancing
northward when on August 9th he met the head of the
Federals at Cedar Run, twenty-five miles north of
Gordonsville (see Sketch 2). The pugnacious Banks
attacked with determination and at first the Confederates were driven back ; then, as at Bull Run, the
Stonewall Brigade came up and checked the rout, after
which Hill's Division drove home a counter-attack.
The Federals, in spite of gallant resistance, were driven
from the field, with heavy loss. Jackson followed up for
a mile or two ; seeing, however, that he might have the
whole of Pope's army on his hands he turned about and
retired to Gordonsville. He could not afford to lose
men by attacking superior forces, but he hoped to lure
Pope southwards ; Lee could then come up, and the
united Confederates would be strong enough to attack.

Pope was eager to push forward but got orders from
Washington to halt on the Rapidan.

On August 13th Lee heard that McClellan was
beginning to embark his troops—this meant that Pope
would soon be reinforced. He therefore left 25,000
at Richmond and took all his other troops to join
Jackson. This gave him 55,000 for an offensive blow.
His intention was to turn Pope's left, but unluckily for
him the Federal cavalry captured an officer bearing
a letter which revealed the plan. Thus warned, Pope
wisely fell back behind the Rappahannock. Though
Stuart brought off another cavalry raid, the position of
the Federals seemed secure ; heavy rain made the river
impassable for some days ; the arrival of troops from
the Peninsula brought their numbers up to 70,000.

Ropes suggests that Pope ought to have been ordered
back to Manassas, and certainly events showed that this
course would have been safer. But Pope can scarcely

be blamed for failing to foresee the daring stroke that
Lee was planning. ' In war men are nothing; it is the
Man who is everything.' Lee was about to provide
a memorable example of the truth of this maxim.

Second Bull Run. Lee had 55,000 men, divided into
two Corps (Jackson and Longstreet). In front of him
lay the Federals, 70,000 strong, with reinforcements
coming up daily. It was evident that the only chance
of success for Lee was in immediate action. But the
river was unfordable and a frontal attack was hopeless.
In these circumstances Lee decided to attack the nerve
centre of his foe—his communications; the object was to
intensify the fog of war so that the physical strength of
the enemy might be expended in aimless wanderings; the
larger an army the more is it thrown into confusion by
sudden changes of plan ; the oftener plans are changed
the more do men lose confidence in their leaders ; while
the leaders, afraid of striking blows at nothing, hesitate
and waste time before taking vigorous action.

The best part of Lee's strategy lay in the fact that
there were no half measures about it ; this was no
cavalry raid to capture stores and cut a railway ; it was
a game for big stakes.

Before dawn on August 25th, Jackson, with Stuart's
cavalry and his own Corps, started on a long flank march
right round to the westward (see Sketch 10). A march
of twenty-five miles brought him to Salem. Again,
before dawn on the next day, the troops were in motion
by Thorofare Gap, Gainesville, and then south-east to
Bristoe Station. The whole of Pope's force now lay
directly between the two wings of Lee's army.

The Confederates spent the 27th in a joyous pillage
of the huge stores at Manassas. On the 28th detachments were sent north as far as Centreville, after which
Jackson collected his men in the woods near Groveton,
to await the arrival of Longstreet.

It is not surprising that Pope was bewildered. On the 25th Longstreet was keeping up a demonstration on the south of the Rappahannock; reports were received that some Confederates were moving to the north-west, but it was believed that their destination was the Valley. On the 26th it was known that Jackson had crossed Thorofare, which made Pope turn to the north. On the 27th Jackson was located at Manassas, and Pope turned in that direction, hoping to catch this wing of Lee's army. But when he arrived at Manassas on the 28th the birds had flown ; the next news of them was at Centreville and there was nothing for it but to follow. By this time the various counter orders had tied Pope's army into knots. With some difficulty three Corps were got to Centreville on the evening of the 28th only to find the birds had flown again.

August 28th. The safe course for Pope was to collect his scattered forces behind the Bull Run and take up a defensive position ; this would have left Jackson with nothing but the stores at Manassas to show as trophies after all this manœuvring.

But an important incident took place on the evening of the 28th. One of the scattered Federal Divisions (King's) was making its way from Gainesville to Centreville ; out of the woods on its left burst the Confederates, and a fierce but indecisive battle was waged for a couple of hours near the village of Groveton. This attack was a brilliant move on the part of Jackson ; he knew that Longstreet was already in Thorofare Gap, barely twelve miles away, and he wanted to lure the Confederates back to the south side of the Bull Run. Pope, who with all his faults was a fighting general, fell into the trap ; he read the report from King as indicating that Jackson, having completed his raid, was now only anxious to escape, and was fighting his way back to the Gap; there was a hope of defeating him at once.

Orders were issued for all Corps to attack Jackson on the 29th.

August 29th. The Confederates had taken up a line along the embankment of an unfinished railway, with their left on the Bull Run (see Sketch 11). On the Federal side the confusion had been too great to be straightened out at once ; the troops from Centreville did not reach the field till after midday and the assaults were disjointed and failed to break the line. Porter's Corps, which had been wandering about Manassas, was ordered to form the extreme left at Gainesville ; about three miles short of that place it came face to face with Longstreet's Corps ; the two forces remained opposite each other for the rest of the day and took no part in the battle which was going on to the north of them.

August 30th. Pope still believed that Longstreet had not come up, and, therefore, as the Federal forces were now well in line, he resumed the attempt to crush Jackson. It was a purely frontal attack on the line of the railway embankment. The Confederates made the most of this natural parapet, which had a fine field of fire 500 yards to the front. The Federal assaults gained a footing once or twice, but only with shattered forces which were thrown out again by counter-strokes.

Then Lee sent Longstreet's fresh Corps to attack the enemy's left from the south, and the result was decisive. The Federals fell back, and with some difficulty got across the Bull Run.

The casualties were heavy on both sides, the North lost nearly 15,000, and the South 10,000.

Pope's army fell back behind the forts of Washington.

XI

ANTIETAM

DURING the last half of August troops had been coming up from Fort Monroe and were sent on to join Pope. On the 27th McClellan himself arrived at Alexandria ; he had now only two Corps left of his command, those of Franklin and Sumner, but even these were without transport and artillery horses. As the news of Jackson's raid on Manassas began to arrive, Halleck wanted these Corps sent quickly in that direction. He and McClellan bungled the arrangements between them (with more bad temper on each side), and neither Franklin nor Sumner reached Pope till the battle was over, though it is pretty clear that they might have done so. McClellan created a bad impression by saying that ' Pope must be left to get out of his scrape as best he could ' ; no doubt he meant that the man on the spot is the best informed and can disentangle the mess better than anybody else ; if another officer were sent to supersede him it would only add to the confusion. But it was an unfortunate way of putting it, and, taken in conjunction with the delay about Franklin and Sumner, it left the impression that McClellan was not doing his best.

On the 30th the news became alarming—Pope was retiring, and the situation was much as it had been a year earlier after the First Bull Run.

On September 3rd Lincoln made one of the big decisions of his life—to place McClellan in command of all the troops at Washington. Stanton, Chase, Halleck were violently opposed to such an idea ; they judged McClellan by the tone of his letters and found him dangerous ; he had returned from the Peninsula under a cloud, and had just given grounds for suspicion that he was leaving a brother officer in the lurch.

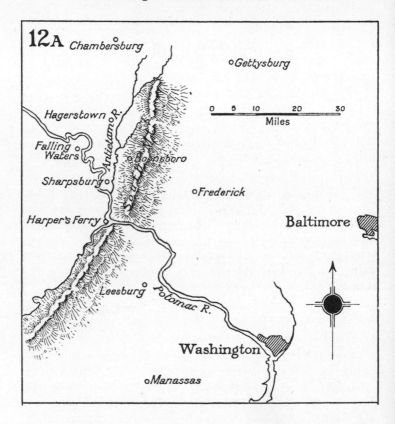

COUNTRY ROUND THE ANTIETAM

Lincoln, in his usual direct manner, went straight to the heart of the trouble ; chaos was spreading to an extent which foreboded disaster ; chaos can only be cured by organization ; organization demands one man, not several, in supreme control ; McClellan had shown once before his power of control ; therefore, McClellan must be installed with an absolutely free hand to take command of chaos.

This did not imply that Lincoln had in any way changed his opinion of the general ; he told his secretary that ' if McClellan could not fight himself he could teach others how to fight '—and this was all that mattered. It showed that he could act in opposition to his Cabinet, a fact which has important bearing on later events. It also showed that he could rise calmly above the atmosphere of personal intrigues, petty jealousies, and slanderous accusations, which had filled Washington.

It is going too far to say that McClellan saved the Capital itself ; there were over 140,000 troops within the circle of the forts, and at least 30,000 of these had not yet been engaged. Lee, with less than half this number, never dreamt of making an attack. But it is true that McClellan's organizing powers were of real value, as Lincoln had foreseen. Chaos was soon put straight ; the garrisons of the forts were rearranged ; stragglers were collected and sent back to their regiments ; the confidence of the population was restored. In less than a week a field army of 85,000 was put on the move. McClellan decided to take command of it himself, although he got no orders on this subject.

It was indeed time for the Federal forces to be moving. Lee had crossed the Potomac and on September 7th was reported to be at Frederick (forty miles N. by W. of Washington). He might move to Baltimore and cut off the Capital from the north, or he might go on into Pennsylvania.

McClellan followed and on September 13th he reached Frederick. There he had the great and un-usual good luck to be put in possession of the plan of the enemy. A private soldier picked up three cigars, wrapped up in a piece of paper which turned out to be

a copy of Lee's orders. They revealed that Lee was
once more dividing his army. Longstreet's Corps was
to march to Boonsboro, and halt : Jackson was to turn
south, cross the Potomac and move on Harper's Ferry,
while two other Divisions were to close on the same
spot from the north and east : after Harper's Ferry was
taken all were to rejoin Longstreet near Boonsboro.

Harper's Ferry was held by 9,000 Federals ; there
were also small garrisons at Winchester and Martinsburg. Strategically it was a sound idea to have a strong
post on the Potomac at the north end of the Valley, and
in addition it protected the important railway bridge
over the river. But tactically it was in the worst
possible site ; there were heights commanding it from
the north, south, and east ; to hold these would require
a large garrison. McClellan had recommended that the
post should be abandoned, and the garrison brought
away to reinforce the field army ; but this had not been
done.

Lee saw that he might have to depend on the Valley
as his line of communications, and it would be dangerous to leave so many of the enemy's troops in his
rear. But Harper's Ferry would be an easy prey, and
the capture of 9,000 men at small expense was a strong
inducement to take it. With his experience of
McClellan's deliberate methods he calculated there
would be time enough for Jackson to carry out his
mission and rejoin before Longstreet could be attacked.
And the calculation would have probably come out right
but for the accident of the lost order.

McClellan had his choice of two courses. First, to
march to the relief of Harper's Ferry ; but even if he
arrived in time he would scarcely be able to catch the
elusive Jackson, who could slip away to the west or
south. Second, leaving Harper's Ferry to its fate, to
attack Longstreet ; even if Longstreet slipped away he
would have to cross the Potomac—and Maryland would

AMBROSE EVERETT BURNSIDE (1824–1881)
Major General, U.S.A.

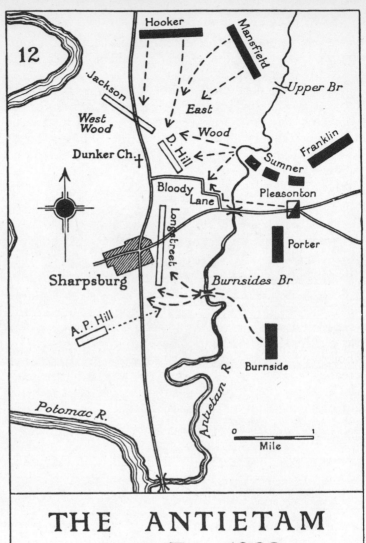

12

Hooker

Mansfield

Upper Br

Jackson

West
Wood

East

Wood

Franklin

Dunker Ch.

D. Hill

Sumner

Pleasonton

Bloody
Lane

Longstreet

Porter

Sharpsburg

Burnsides Br

A. P. Hill

Burnside

Potomac R.

Antietam R.

0   1
Mile

THE ANTIETAM
Sept. 17th., 1862

be free of the enemy's forces. He decided on the second course, but sent one Corps (Franklin's) to see what could be done towards Harper's Ferry.

Though the lost order came into his hands about noon and was accepted as genuine, it did not spur McClellan to any desperate haste ; none of his troops started before daybreak next morning. (Sixteen hours delay ! Jackson would have got his men on the move within one hour.)

September 14th. South Mountain. Immediately in front of the Federal advance the South Mountain formed a serious obstacle. There were only two gaps, but they were not strongly held, and after some hours of tough fighting the Federals gained the crest and the enemy withdrew.

September 15th. Harper's Ferry was surrendered at 8 a.m. Lee was reported to have taken up a line on the west bank of the Antietam, in front of Sharpsburg. It was a sluggish stream with few bridges or fords. The whole Federal Army was within eight miles of that stream at daybreak. After a brief survey of the ground, McClellan spent the rest of the day in preparations and postponed his attack till the 16th.

September 16th. More preparations. Attack postponed till the 17th. The delay was caused by Lee's bold attitude. Though his line on the Antietam was strong, at his rear lay the Potomac, sixty yards wide, no bridge, only one ford—a bad flaw in any defensive position. As McClellan artlessly remarks—'General Lee and I knew each other well. We had served together in Mexico and commanded against each other in the Peninsula. I had the highest respect for his ability as a commander, and knew he was not a general to be trifled with.' Therefore this able general would not commit the crime of standing in a bad position unless he had at least 50,000 men with him. Therefore it was not a time for trifling, and two days were spent in serious preparations for attack. Which was one way of looking at it !

All the same Lee (be it remembered that he and McClellan knew each other well)—Lee had committed the crime of standing there on the 15th with only 20,000. He has been criticized for over-boldness, but the fact remains that it was just this boldness which gained him two days ; and in these two days he was able to collect most of the 50,000 for whom McClellan had given him credit in advance.

September 17th. Antietam (Sharpsburg). In spite of the time taken by McClellan in perfecting his plan, it has not been regarded as a masterpiece. On the evening of the 16th two Corps (Hooker and Mansfield) were sent across the Antietam by the Upper Bridge. (This was a plain intimation that the Federal attack would come from the north, so Jackson was posted to face that way to meet it.) Two more Corps (Sumner and Franklin) were ready to support them. ' As soon as matters looked favourable there ' Burnside's Corps was to make a separate attack on the other flank. If these assaults, or either of them, should prove successful, the centre, with all disposable forces, was to push direct on Sharpsburg.

The right attack was launched by Hooker at 6.0 a.m. after an hour of artillery preparation. It was met by Jackson's two Divisions, and in an hour of desperate combat both sides fought themselves to a standstill. Mansfield took Hooker's place and fought grimly forward, in face of a murderous fire, to West Wood, a few hundred yards north of the Dunker Church. Sumner brought one Division in support. Till 10.30 the battle surged to and fro in attack and counter-attack, but the Federals could not establish themselves any farther forward.

At 9 a.m. Burnside, on the left, got orders to advance, but had not even located the fords and bridge. Much time was wasted, and it was not till 1 p.m. that the Federals gained a footing on the west bank. By 3 p.m. they had fought their way, against a thin line, to the very outskirts of Sharpsburg. At this moment a heavy and quite unexpected attack hit them on their left flank. This came from the Division of A. P. Hill, which had just arrived from Harper's Ferry, doing seventeen miles in eight hours. Hill struck hard, and the Federals, thrown into confusion, fell back to the bridge.

Meanwhile the central attack had begun at 10 a.m. and lasted three hours. It was carried out by two Divisions of Sumner's Corps, with some assistance from Franklin. Over the ' Bloody Lane ', no need to say what happened there, stubbornly forward as far as the turnpike road—but it was only a handful of survivors who got so far. No supports, and they could get no farther, though they had really broken the centre of the Confederate line, had they but known it. The battle died away.

Critics have pointed out that the attacks were disjointed and badly supported : that Porter's Corps was never engaged, and only a small part of Franklin's took part. But the men fought bravely, witness their 12,000 casualties, and they also fought skilfully, witness the 9,000 casualties of the Confederates.

On the 18th September Lee (who knew McClellan well) stood on the bank of the Antietam, and McClellan (who knew Lee well) stood fast on the other bank. After this the Confederates slipped away in the night across the Potomac, and the brief invasion of the North was over.

McClellan made no attempt to follow ; for the moment he was content with having saved Maryland. He spread patrols along the Potomac to watch against any renewal of Lee's attempts, and reoccupied the heights on the north side of Harper's Ferry. Then he set to work to get his army in order for an advance into Virginia. After a halt of six weeks he crossed the Potomac, but when his army had got as far as Warrenton, on November 7th, he received an order to hand over command to Burnside.

Note.—McClellan accepted the famous 'Lost Order' as genuine, and history proves that he was right in doing so.

It is rather curious that in this war, where both sides used clever devices to mislead the enemy, the 'lost order trick' does not seem to have been brought into play. It is an old game—we get a good example of it from Frederick the Great : after defeating the Austrians at Liegnitz (Aug. 15th, 1760) he sent a letter to his brother to say he was marching against the Russians : he had no intention of doing anything of the sort, but the letter was to be intercepted by the Russians, and it actually had the desired effect of making them clear off.

In the Great War, during the retreat from Mons, several British officers 'lost' orders. For instance, an officer was ordered to hold a particular point in the picket line with one company : he 'lost' an order which told him to hold it with a complete battalion and a battery—hoping that if the Germans picked it up they would be shy about attacking, and thus his company would get a night's rest. I have reason to believe that our French brothers-in-arms were playing the same game. It is impossible to say whether there were any results, and of course before long the Germans must have seen through the hoax. But even so no harm was done, for if by chance a genuine order fell into their hands they would look upon it as another hoax and thus it would have no value.

XII

THE MULES OF FREDERICK

McCLELLAN'S dismissal has been the subject of much controversy and deserves serious attention, because it is really the Test Case of Lincoln's strategy. The invasion of the North had been forced back. What was now required was decisive victory over the Confederate forces. Was McClellan the man to win it ? If so, Lincoln made the mistake of his life.

It has been alleged that McClellan, for political reasons, was not wholehearted in his desire for victory. This is the first point to be considered.

A man of intelligence cannot help having political views of some kind, and in America at that time the views were of various different kinds. An able journalist had preached the doctrine that ' no good could come of a Union pinned together by bayonets ' : other people wanted the Union but believed conquest to be impossible, and therefore looked to conciliation and compromise as the only solution : others again wanted complete victory but doubted whether Lincoln and his Cabinet were the men to achieve it. There may have been (in fact, of course, there were) people whose private interests and ambitions coloured their views, but there were plenty of honest men who, loathing war. and especially fratricidal war, looked for a compromise that would end it. Such men were not traitors.

A soldier is in a very different position. Once he puts on uniform his sole duty is to defeat the enemies of that uniform. For him there is no such thing as half loyalty —anything short of wholehearted determination to crush the enemy is treachery. It is said that Lee had difficulty in making up his mind which way duty called him, but once he had put on the Confederate grey there was nothing half-hearted about his fighting.

In McClellan's case good evidence, though indirect, is again to be found in his book. Every page shows the delight he found in his popularity, the cheers of his men, the success of his first appearance in Washington, the flags captured from the enemy. He knew what pleasure such things would give his young wife, and his letters to her betray a vanity which is too boyish to be really offensive. It is not difficult to see, in the margin of those pages, the roseate dreams in which he was indulging. Napoleon, before Marengo, had burst out of the clouds of the Alps on the rear of the Austrians— in like manner another hero would burst out of the mists of ocean and spread consternation in the ranks of the rebels, would take their Capital, destroy their army, save the Union. Well—no harm in dreams like these 'if you can dream and not make dreams your master'. The robust Bard of Avon lived before the days of cant and culture, and had no shame in making Henry V say 'if it is a sin to covet honour I am the most offending soul alive'. But McClellan had reached the dangerous stage where dreams had mastered him. We see the same thing in Napoleon : in 1813 the Allies offered him peace and the fair realm of France, but his dreams of glory would not be satisfied with accepting terms, however generous—he must dictate his own terms ; in fact, the idol of an army does not talk of terms, he simply issues orders. Napoleon really believed that he was France, that France's welfare lay in his glory, and he lost himself in such dreams. In something of the same way McClellan's self-importance had grown to such an extent that he looked upon himself as the only hope of the North, an embodiment of the Union ; any doubts about his wisdom, any criticism of his plans were treason. Let them leave him and the Army of the Potomac alone and all would be well. When a man has dreams like these no incomplete victory will satisfy him. It is impossible to believe that McClellan would have sacrificed one leaf of his expected laurels for any political consideration.

And yet it must be admitted that his indiscretions and delays were quite enough to create a contrary impression; there is also one piece of evidence against him which looks black. While his wrath was hot against Stanton, a tempter appeared in the Peninsula: this was Fernando Wood, Mayor of New York, an advocate of conciliation and a strong Democrat. It is easy to imagine how, after some preliminary abuse of the Government, he worked on the impressionable mind of McClellan, holding out prospects of the Presidency. After the interview McClellan was foolish enough to write a letter, intended for Wood, in which he pledged himself to conduct the war in such a way as to conciliate the South. The actual terms of that letter have never been revealed, but there may be a dim reflection of it in a letter which he wrote to Lincoln soon afterwards; this was a sort of political sermon on the general policy of the North, written 'on the brink of eternity' and dated July 7th. 'This rebellion has assumed the character of a war; as such it should be regarded, and it should be conducted on the highest principles known to Christian civilization.'

The original letter was no doubt stronger than this, and was so indiscreet that General W. F. Smith, to whom it was shown, remonstrated that 'it looked like treason'—and it was not sent. After Antietam, Wood appeared again and this time got the letter. But I think he was mistaken in his man; to Wood's mind 'the highest principles of Christian civilization' meant letting the enemy escape with a view to a patched-up peace; to McClellan's mind they meant chivalrous conduct, kindness to prisoners, prevention of pillage, avoidance of threats—all of which are quite compatible with a desire for decisive victory. The surest means of conciliation would be for the victor to dictate generous terms to the vanquished—*parcere subiectis*—but first he must ascend to the very summit, in order to bring out the full measure of his condescension. Besides this the sweetest revenge on Stanton and Chase would be to return in triumph and receive their forced congratulations.

When the letter was finally given General Smith asked to be allowed to resign. At first sight this looks like a proof of treason, but the fact that it was shown to Smith at all is very significant. W. F. Smith was an officer of the North, which is to say he would have been horror-struck if he believed the letter to be really treasonable, and would have refused to serve for one hour under the commander who could write it. He said it *looked* like treason—a piece of egregious folly (and we know what folly McClellan could write), inspired by personal hatred of Stanton, which might be misread and might cause infinite mischief. He persuaded McClellan to withdraw it and they remained on friendly terms. When the letter was finally given he came to the conclusion that co-operation between McClellan and the Government was hopeless; in such circumstances success in the field was hopeless; so he took the only course that was open to show McClellan a strong protest against such obstinate folly.

One more argument—McClellan was a soldier. Soldiers may be conceited, and petulant, and obstinate, and even disobedient—but the other thing isn't done.

Politics. A man may be true to the uniform of his country but thoroughly opposed to its Government. And we can give McClellan credit for using no ambi-

guous terms about this. There were letters sufficient
to put him in front of a court martial. He was known
to be a Democrat (though perhaps he hardly knew it
himself) and opposed to the Emancipation project
which Lincoln was just bringing out. There was a
clique at Washington, including Stanton, Chase, and
Halleck, who wanted to be rid of him. It has generally
been assumed that Lincoln gave way to their pressure.
The evidence in favour of this assumption, though not
definite, is certainly strong. On the other side there is
only what we know of Lincoln.

Able writers who have analysed Lincoln agree that
he was at once simple and complex, but on the simple
side there seem to be three outstanding traits. First,
of course, his determination to maintain the Union,
which governed everything else. Second : he was free
from personal animosity to such an extent that he
employed those whom he knew to be personal enemies
as long as he thought them useful to the Union : for
instance, Stanton had been a virulent and outspoken
critic of the administration—Lincoln made him Secretary for War. Third : one of the few things that
aroused his anger was any suggestion that he was influenced by politics in making military appointments.

Apply these ruling principles to the case of McClellan,
and it follows that Lincoln was not afraid of his politics :
pressure from politicians would only incline him to
stick to McClellan as he had done once before. The
only test he applied to a general was whether he could
and would defeat the rebels. The assumption that
Lincoln gave way to political pressure is an accusation
of weakness in the one spot where he was—well, I won't
say strong, but 'cussed perverse'. He listened, as was
his way, to what Stanton and others had to say, but
the decision was his own.

This narrows down the discussion to the question
whether the decision was based on treachery or in-

competence. Of course, he heard reports about the former, and they may have prompted a visit which he paid McClellan ; he went to Antietam and spent four days there ostensibly to look at the battle-field and inspect the troops, probably with the deeper object of inspecting the general. There were long consultations and discussions in a cordial tone. McClellan says :

' He more than once assured me that he was fully satisfied with my whole course ; that the only fault he could find was that I was too prone to be sure that everything was ready before starting, but that my actions were all right when I started.' . . . ' He would stand by me against all comers.' . . . ' I have no doubt he meant exactly what he said.'

Lincoln meant what he said, and there is also a deduction to be made from what he left unsaid. It was ever his way to speak out to men when he had suspicions against them ; on a former occasion, March 8th, he had frankly told McClellan that there were people who regarded the Fort Monroe plan as a treacherous movement, to get the defenders away from Washington and so deliver the Capital to the enemy. If he had any suspicions left on October 4th, when they parted, he would surely have spoken about them. It seems fair to assume that McClellan's conversation, which was always free, satisfied him on this point : the general's delight over the ' glorious success at Antietam ', his pride in his army, left no doubt about his will and intention to pursue the path of glory. The only remaining doubt was whether the procrastination, which Lincoln had vainly tried to overcome in the Peninsula, would again paralyse the army. There was a hope that McClellan had learnt something from his first failure.

Lincoln uttered a warning and, to avoid any misunderstanding, followed it up with a definite order. This order was dated October 5th. The one dismissing McClellan was dated November 5th. It is very probable that Lincoln had fixed in his own mind a time

limit of one month as a test ; he had a habit of fixing
beforehand the time for taking certain action. If in
that month McClellan fought a battle, or made a real
attempt to force a battle on Lee, he would be retained
in command ; if it was to be a repetition of the
Peninsula, preparations for to-morrow, absolute disregard for orders—then he must go.

The worst forebodings were more than realized. In
the last fifty pages of McClellan's book we get his
views, during that month. He describes the troops
whose ' decisive victory ' he had just been glorifying :
in some cases ' the morale had been a good deal impaired
in those severely contested actions '. There was de-
ficiency in horses, transport, clothing. ' This army is
not now in condition to undertake another campaign nor
to bring on another battle unless great advantages are
offered by some mistake of the enemy.' Apparently the
morale of the South had not been impaired by defeat
for ' I rather apprehend a renewal of the attempt
in Maryland '. And then ' There are indications of
heavy reinforcements moving toward the enemy '.

The complaints about various deficiencies may have
been justified, and a general cannot be blamed for
wanting his army to be well equipped. But the whole
tone of his letters was unmistakable. ' The mules of
Frederick the Great went through twenty campaigns
and still remained mules.' McClellan had been
through the Peninsula and Antietam—and was more
mulish than ever ; capable of good strong work in his
own way and at his own pace ; serenely contemptuous
of any guiding rein ; while a definite order, like a whip
to a mule, only made him plant his toes in the ground.
He refused to believe that the Government wanted to
help, they were still the enemy in the rear, while the
enemy in front was in overwhelming numbers—' of
course '. Such was the impression on Lincoln—so at
the end of the month McClellan was dismissed.

So much have most authors accepted the view that the dismissal was on political grounds that they have scarcely troubled to discuss it on military grounds. Briefly, the view is that McClellan's successor was worse, and therefore Lincoln was wrong : an honest soldier, who had twice saved Washington, was thrown to the political wolves who had long been howling for his blood ; and we are expected to join in shedding a manly tear over the victim.

My own views might appear to be partial—which they are. Better therefore to quote from some authors who cannot be accused of any tenderness towards Lincoln. Here are some opinions of McClellan :

Ropes, vol. ii, p. 105. ' McClellan was neither an enterprising man nor a ' fighting ' general. He had a constitutional aversion to the risks inseparable from all military operations.' P. 241 ' It was inexcusable for McClellan to state such a preposterous estimate of the size of Lee's army.' P. 359 'With these badly conceived and ill-combined movements did General McClellan begin the battle of the Antietam.'

Not a fighting man—inexcusable in exaggerating the numbers of the enemy—a poor tactician—well, well !

Henderson, vol. ii, p. 278. ' Lee and Jackson had no reason to respect the Union army as a weapon of offence, and very great reason to believe that McClellan was incapable of wielding it.' P. 279 ' McClellan had still to grasp the elementary rule that the combination of superior numbers and of all arms against a single point is necessary to win battles.'

It makes us rub our eyes to read, a few pages farther on, that the dismissal of such a general was a 'deplorable blunder '. Perhaps Lee—he and McClellan knew each other very well—perhaps Lee deplored the dismissal of his old friend.

My conclusions may be summed up.

1. Lincoln, after much deliberation, had arrived at the same opinion as Ropes and Henderson—that McClellan was not fit for the command of an army

intended for offensive operations.   This was an all-
sufficient reason for dismissing him.

2. McClellan was incapable of treason and Lincoln
was satisfied on this point. (My conjecture.)

3. There was strong political pressure applied, but
Lincoln would have ' stuck to McClellan against all
comers ' if he had thought him a competent general.

Some of these conclusions, which are not in accordance with certain evidence, are based on my idea
of the mentality of the two men : my idea of Lincoln is
taken from Lord Charnwood's book, which is sympathetic and very convincing ; that of McClellan from
his own book —equally convincing.

XIII

EMANCIPATION

ON September 23rd, four days after Antietam, Lincoln issued the famous Proclamation that on the 1st January 1863, ' all persons held as slaves within any State, the people whereof shall then be in rebellion against the United States, shall be thenceforward and forever free '. This has been universally recognized as one of the great Charters of Freedom, and due reverence is paid to Lincoln as the author of it. But the actual form and the date of issue were dictated by military necessity.

In normal times the President had no power to free a single slave. But in time of war a commander-in-chief can seize and dispose of the property of the enemy, such as horses and wagons ; as the South looked on their slaves in the same light as on horses, they could be seized and disposed of. This, however, could only apply to the property of those who were in rebellion. In the case of the Northern and border States, Lincoln could only appeal to the State Legislatures to introduce emancipation. This he did persistently, suggesting various schemes for compensation, but his efforts were not successful.

The Proclamation was therefore the act of the Commander-in-Chief, and a real part of his strategy ; it is from this point of view that we must consider it.

Man Power. Volunteer recruiting had fallen to a low ebb. At the outset of the Peninsular Campaign the recruiting offices had been closed ; after the Seven Days they were reopened, and a call was made for 300,000 men, but the response was poor. It must be remembered that business was unusually brisk, especially in the industrial centres, and there was the temptation to remain at home and make money instead of risking life in the field ; to those who had families to support the temptation was strong.

A scheme was now put forward to raise battalions of emancipated slaves. By the end of 1863 there were 100,000 of them under arms, and by the end of the war this number had risen to 180,000. They were rarely employed in the field, but were used as garrisons, railway guards, fatigue parties, and on other duties behind the line, which freed a large number of white men for service at the front.

At the same time the South was deprived of the labour of the negroes who escaped—a very serious deprivation at a time when the Confederacy was so badly in need of men. This step was therefore a real advantage to the North from the military point of view.

Foreign Opinion. The second military reason for the step was that Lincoln had resolved to bar the way to anything like an intervention or an armistice or a compromise. Perhaps more than any man he looked forward to peace, but he believed that a peace at this moment could not be a lasting one. He saw that the disease from which America was suffering lay too deep to be cured by soothing balms ; the surgeon must use the knife and cut out the disease at its root. The disease was secession, arising from the constitutional canker of slavery, and before a lasting peace could come these two questions must be settled definitely and for ever. With the calculation of a true strategist, he saw that this could be done, and he was grimly determined to prosecute the war to the end. The Proclamation was a strategic move to forestall the efforts of peacemakers at home and abroad.

There was real danger of intervention from England and France. It would at first take the form of an offer of mediation ; if the North refused, the European Powers would then recognize the Confederacy and break the blockade. After Second Bull Run it was the general belief that the North could never subdue the South, and that lives were being sacrificed in a hopeless cause—a belief that was shared by many Americans although they could not express themselves so freely. Lord John Russell [1] brought up the matter in the British Cabinet, and there is no reason to doubt that he did so honestly ' in the interests of peace and humanity ' ; it is true that there were also the material interests of cotton spinners and merchants—and it is the duty of a British Government to watch over British interests.

But when the Proclamation established Abolition as a definite issue of the war, the North could insist upon it as an indispensable condition before accepting an offer of mediation, and the British Government could not refuse to admit it. The South, however eager for peace, would not accept intervention with Abolition tacked on.

Yet, though the Proclamation stopped active measures by the British Government, it did not arouse immediate sympathy in the nation. And this is not surprising if we examine the construction put upon it by the clever propagandists of the South. They quoted Lincoln's own words : ' If I could save the Union without freeing any slave, I would do it ; if I could save it by freeing all the slaves, I would do it ; and if I could do it by freeing some and leaving others alone, I would also do that. What I do about the coloured race I do because I believe it would help to save the Union.'

[1] Lord John was created Earl Russell in 1861, but, as one of the wits of the day remarked, he will always be known in history by his maiden name.

Seward had gone even farther than this, instructing
the American Ministers abroad to explain that no attack
was threatened on slavery. The Proclamation itself
gave freedom to slaves of the rebel States, but did
not touch those of the States that were faithful to
the Union. Very naturally the British, ignorant of
American law, thought that if the President could
emancipate the slaves of the South, he could do the
same for those of the North, and they were easily persuaded that he was cynically indifferent to the condition
of the negroes and only thirsted for vengeance on
their owners. The London *Spectator* said: ' The
Proclamation has been made in a way that takes from it
half its usefulness and almost all its grace. The
principle at stake is entirely disregarded, and emancipation promised as a mere incident in the war.' A strong
sympathizer with the North wrote : ' Is it not natural
that those unacquainted with American politics should
be puzzled by the Proclamation which leaves the slaves
of the loyal in slavery ? ' England has long since
given Lincoln the honour that was his due, but at the
time she could scarcely be expected to show herself
plus royaliste que le roi by hailing as a Charter of
Humanity the step which its author put forward as
a measure of war expediency. The opportunism ob-
scured the deeper meaning.

But the Proclamation spiked the British guns, and
that was what the Strategist wanted at the moment.

The Opposition. Of course a large section of the
public in the North hailed emancipation with deep
satisfaction, and supported Lincoln with fresh enthusiasm. At the same time the way was opened to a
revival of party politics which had been in abeyance.
First Bull Run had awakened Americans to the fact
that the rebellion was a serious attempt to break up the
Union which they loved ; this was quite enough to

ensure honest support for a Government that was determined to crush that rebellion. The disappointments of the year '62 stirred up suspicion that the Government, though good in its intentions, was bad in the execution of them. The malcontents were not yet bold enough to say openly that the rebellion could not be crushed, but those who coveted the sweets of office began to look for a platform from which they could abuse the Government without incurring the reproach of treason or weakness. Lincoln's Proclamation was of use to them : they put the Union flag in the foreground and protested their loyalty, but demanded ' the Union as it was ', and went on to denounce the Proclamation as unconstitutional, its author as a usurper. Once the voice of opposition was let loose, there were plenty of minor complaints to swell its noise : public money was being wasted ; the call for recruits was unfair on certain States ; and so forth.

In October and November some elections took place and all the bitterness of party spirit was called into them. Five of the principal States turned against the Government, and the strength of the Democrats became a real threat. Had they obtained an absolute majority they could have refused to vote money for the war, and such action would have brought it to an end. Curiously enough it was the support of the Border States, where slavery still existed, that saved the Government.

From this date, however, there was, in Congress and the press, a declared opposition, with all its inherent traditions. The extreme section was known as 'Copperheads ' ; one of its leaders was a certain Vallandigham and his words, spoken in Congress in January 1863, show the extent to which the opposition could go.

' The war for the Union is in your hands a most bloody and costly failure. War for the Union was abandoned, war for the negro openly begun. With what success ? Let the dead at Fredericksburg answer. Ought this war to continue ? I answer

no—not a day, not an hour. What then ? Shall we separate ?
Again I answer no, no, no. Stop fighting. Make an armistice.
Accept at once foreign mediation.'

There were two particular measures which the agita-
tors hastened to label as unconstitutional and tyrannical
—conscription and martial law.

Conscription. The gradual building up of the Union
Army has not been followed in these pages because in
a war of nations recruiting is the business of the statesman rather than of the strategist. The general in the
field wants as many men as he can get. It is for the
statesman to supply them. He wants to avoid too
sudden a drain on the industries which maintain
existence and furnish the wealth of the country ;
naturally the first expedient is to call for volunteers ;
to this there is a ready response from youths who have
little to lose and are not settled in life. Later on the
citizen who has responsibilities at home must weigh
them against the sense of duty to his country. Gradually
the time comes when the system of purely voluntary
service is inadequate. It is interesting to note that in
England this stage was reached after a couple of years in
the Great War—it was the same in the North.

Compulsory service became law on the 3rd March
1863 ; it did not abolish the voluntary system and was
only put into force in the districts which were unable
to supply the quota for which they were responsible.
The organization, which had hitherto been in the
hands of State Governors, was now controlled directly
from Washington ; provost marshals were appointed
to every district ; they made out rolls of all able-
bodied men between the ages of twenty and forty-five.
After taking such volunteers as presented themselves,
the balance of the quota was filled up by lot from those
who were liable to serve.

Conscription acted as a strong stimulus to volunteering. The Government was already offering a bounty of

300 dollars to each volunteer ; this was increased by the States and Counties, which were anxious to fill their quota without resorting to compulsion. In some States the total bounty was over 600 dollars for each recruit. This gave rise to the abuse known as ' bounty jumping '—a man volunteered, took his bounty, deserted, changed his name, and then volunteered again. Another abuse came from substitutes : the law allowed a conscript to get off by providing a substitute ; this was carried on to such a degree that regular 'substitute brokers ' came into existence. The market price of a substitute was about 1,000 dollars. The bounty jumpers and paid substitutes, vagabonds of the country, were worthless as soldiers.

When the figures are examined [1] it appears that conscripts and substitutes were very few in number compared with volunteers—and the real effect of the Conscription Law was to stimulate volunteering. But it gave the opposition a topic for further eloquence about tyranny, and promoted some riots by men who resisted the draft.

Martial Law. On the 24th September 1862, the President issued a Proclamation suspending the writ of *Habeas Corpus* in the case of persons arrested for treasonable practices ; this amounted to imposing Martial Law on the whole country. Many people were imprisoned, including the notorious Vallandigham. It goes without saying that the malcontents denounced this measure as illegal and its administration as harsh and unfair. The Bastille is always a good subject for an agitator.

Effects of Emancipation. The opposition started on wide topics—violation of the Constitution, usurpation

---

[1] Rhodes, vol. vi, p. 426. ' According to the report of the Provost-Marshal-General of March 17th, 1866, there were held to service (i. e. conscripted) 9,881, furnished substitutes 26,002.'

of power, waste of blood and money; then went on to abuse individuals—Lincoln was doing nothing; he was doing too much; at all events he was doing wrong.

The military student, however, need not attempt to weigh the political effects; it is enough for us to know that the votes of the public supported Lincoln and he was able to weather some pretty bad storms. There can be no doubt about the weight of the military results. The way was barred to foreign intervention and this was perhaps a decisive factor in the war.

XIV

FREDERICKSBURG

The Command.

BURNSIDE had been selected to succeed in the command, and the appointment was not a success. This has been urged as an argument that McClellan should have been retained. Ropes says : ' McClellan ought not to have been removed unless the Government were prepared to put in his place some officer whom they knew to be at least his equal in military capacity.' There are some qualifications which can be tested to a certain extent in peace time, such as knowledge, judgement, energy, and power of command. But the crowning qualification for a Commander-in-Chief is the nerve which can bear heavy responsibility, and this can only be tested in the fire of actual warfare. I think this had been brought home to Lincoln by the strain of responsibility that lay on his own shoulders. At all events he seems to have been guided in his selections by a simple rule of thumb—to pick the man who had done something in an independent capacity. McClellan, Halleck, Pope, Burnside, Grant were all selected on this principle. In the case of the first four, the choice turned out badly because Lincoln had very little to go on.

At this moment the choice seemed to lie between Burnside (who was the senior), Sumner (a fine soldier but rather too old), Franklin, and Hooker. Burnside had held command in some minor operations which had been planned, with the assistance of the navy, to shut up the ports on the coast of Carolina; his success there earned him the promotion. Besides this, there was another recommendation which at this moment had considerable weight—he was not associated with either side in the recriminations which followed the disaster of Second Bull Run ; a very bitter feeling had sprung up between officers of the Army of the Potomac and those of Pope's army ; McClellan's removal might have accentuated the feeling unless his successor had sufficient tact to suppress it. Burnside was a personal friend of McClellan but had not been present either in the Peninsula or at Second Bull Run and had not quarrelled with anybody. He was known to be a man of much personal charm, and this is proved by the fact that though his failure cost him his reputation as a soldier, it did not affect the esteem in which he was held.

He was not eager, in fact he was very unwilling, to accept the appointment, but, as Rhodes points out, this was probably more of a recommendation than otherwise in the eyes of Lincoln ; the great Washington himself had said : ' I do not think myself equal to the command I am honoured with.' Burnside's modesty, after the cocksure self-assertion of McClellan, must have made him a very much easier colleague to work with.

November 1862. The Union forces were about Warrenton when, on November 7th, Burnside took command. He knew that Longstreet's Corps was in front of him at Culpeper, while Jackson was still in the Valley. McClellan's plan had been to move against Longstreet, hoping to bring him to battle before Jackson could come up. From what we know of Lee and his lieutenants it seems very unlikely that Longstreet would have been caught by McClellan's deliberate methods ; more likely the Federals would have been drawn farther southward, lengthening and weakening their line of communications which would then present another opportunity to Jackson. Such was Burnside's view, and he changed the plan entirely.

Instead of advancing against Longstreet, he proposed to move by Fredericksburg. The advantages of this line were considerable : it was the most direct road to the Southern Capital and made use of the Potomac as far as Acquia Creek, thus shortening the communications which had been so vulnerable. It was hoped that Fredericksburg might be seized before the enemy realized the danger to it. The objection to the plan was that it left Jackson free to make another dash northwards. Washington, however, was by this time well guarded, and the Potomac presented a serious obstacle in winter. Burnside's plan was submitted to the President who gave his assent : ' He thinks ', wrote Halleck, ' that it will succeed if you move quickly, otherwise not.'

Unfortunately there was nothing like rapidity in the execution. The pontoons which were required for building bridges did not arrive in time, owing to some very bad staff work. Further delay was entailed by repairs to the railway track.

On November 17th the leading troops under Sumner arrived at Falmouth, opposite Fredericksburg ; as the Confederates had a very weak force on the spot, Sumner could have crossed and secured the heights on the south bank ; but Burnside would not allow this until the bridges were ready, for fear of having Sumner cut off on the south bank. It was not until the 25th that pontoons were available, and as Longstreet's Corps had arrived on the 21st strong opposition was now to be expected. On the 30th Jackson's Corps came in to bring the Confederates up to full strength.

When all chance of effecting a surprise had vanished, Burnside seems to have lost his head. He had not sufficient imagination to devise any scheme but a simple frontal attack. He had not the strength of

JAMES LONGSTREET (1821–1904)
Lieutenant General, C.S.A.

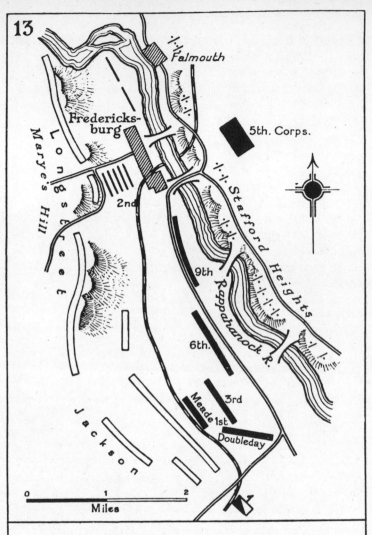

FREDERICKSBURG
Dec. 13th., 1862

mind to give up his plan when the altered conditions
made it dangerous, and yet he had not the strength
to carry it on with resolution. Consequently the
battle of Fredericksburg can be summed up in few
words—a frontal attack against a well-prepared position; rarely has less manœuvre or finesse been seen in
a general engagement.

Fredericksburg. 13th December 1862. Lee had taken
up a position on the ridge running parallel to the
Rappahannock, a mile or more from the bank. Longstreet's Corps held Marye's Hill, immediately above
the town, and since November 21st had been busy
improving the line. Jackson's Corps had been spread
out to the east, to watch the lower reach of the river,
but was now drawn in to get close touch with the right
of Longstreet. Their united strength was just under
80,000 and the front was six miles long.

On the north bank the Stafford Heights ran close
along the river, and on these Burnside placed 150 heavy
guns to cover the crossing. It was no doubt on account
of these guns that Lee made no attempt to dispute
the passage; he was content to await attack farther
back.

Sumner commanded the right wing, 2nd and 9th
Corps, with orders to move against the town. The
1st and 6th Corps under Franklin formed the left, two
miles to the east. Hooker had the 3rd and 5th Corps
in reserve. Total 120,000.

On December 11th pontoon bridges were thrown
across and the town was taken after some sharp fighting.
Next day the whole of Sumner's and Franklin's troops
moved over and a council was held to consider further
action. Franklin proposed to attack the Confederate
right, which seemed their weakest point, with a force
of 40,000 men. Burnside, however, could not make
up his mind to so great a risk. It may be, and probably

is, true that if more men had been thrown in the only result would have been to increase the casualties ; but the sole advantage of the Federals lay in their superior numbers, and it is obvious that this advantage disappears if the whole strength is not made use of. It certainly demanded much courage on the part of the commander to throw his full strength against so strong a line ; more courage perhaps to abandon a hopeless plan and retire. Burnside took the middle course. After much delay orders were issued for Sumner and Franklin to send forward one division each, while the remaining divisions were to be ' held in readiness to support the movement strongly '.

If there was hesitation in the issue of orders there was no hesitation in the gallant effort to carry them out, and I think it was on the bloody field of Fredericksburg that the Northern soldiers rose to the highest pinnacle of their heroism. They had not the consciousness of past victories to inspire them ; the desperate nature of their task must have been apparent to every man ; for a couple of weeks they had been watching the enemy's preparations. A delay in attacking always strains the nerves and weakens confidence in the commander. But if any soldiers could have won the battle, assuredly these men would have done it.

On the left Meade's division, with some support from Doubleday, was sent against Jackson's position, and got into the first line ; but the Confederates had ample reserves to drive them out again with a loss of 5,000. The left attack had failed.

On the other flank Sumner sent forward the 2nd Corps. A mile in front of it lay a road with a stone wall which had been converted into a stout parapet and lined with Southern riflemen. In succession the divisions of Hancock, French, Howard, and later Humphreys were flung against this wall, but never reached it, though they lost over 7,000 men in the fruitless endeavour.

The total Confederate losses were 5,300, most of them in Jackson's Corps, which had been in some hand-to-hand fighting.

Lee has been criticized for not making a counter attack ; it seems, however, that he hoped the Federals would renew their attempt the next day, which certainly would have suited the Confederates best. In his desperation Burnside was ready to do it—he proposed himself to lead his old Corps (the 9th) to the assault, but the Corps commanders succeeded in dissuading him.

The armies lay facing each other during the 14th and 15th, and then during the night the Federals were withdrawn to the north bank.

'History records fortunately but few instances of brave men sent to destruction by the incompetence of their General in a more hopeless undertaking.' [1]

It is only fair to Burnside to record that he made no attempt to throw the blame of this disaster on other shoulders ; in his first account of the battle he accepted entire responsibility. An unpleasant suggestion was made by the enemies of the Government that the letter of penance had been dictated from the Capital with a view to whitewashing Lincoln, but American historians have proved that this had no foundation.

Though Burnside took the blame on himself, it cannot be denied that the President must be given a share of it, he had appointed the General and given assent to his plan. It was an error in judging the human factor, which in time of war is of all things the most difficult to judge. The historian pronounces judgement after the verdict of the battle has been given. It is, however noticeable, that the authors who have been most severe in this matter have only destruc-

[1] Wood and Edmonds, p. 150.

tive criticism to offer, and have not ventured to name any one who, before the battle, had better claims to the appointment.

The verdict of the battle was quite definite enough to make another change necessary in the command, and this was openly voiced in the army itself. The troops lost all confidence in Burnside, desertion was rife and discipline was deteriorating.

The unhappy General made some frantic efforts to resume the offensive ; a movement was attempted up the Rappahannock to turn the Confederate line, but the weather defeated it before any fighting took place. The ' Mud March ', as it was called, completed the discontent, and made Burnside's position intolerable. He insisted that he must resign or else that the Corps commanders should all be removed. Lincoln accepted his resignation, and replaced him with Hooker.

XV

CHANCELLORSVILLE

General J. Hooker.

'FIGHTING Joe Hooker' had gained a well-deserved reputation as a dashing leader in the Peninsula and at Antietam, where he was wounded at the head of his Corps.

We get a good idea of his personality in a celebrated letter he received from Lincoln on his appointment—and it gives us at the same time a glimpse into Lincoln's own mind.

'I have placed you at the head of the Army of the Potomac. Of course I have done this upon what appears to me to be sufficient reasons, and yet I think it best for you to know that there are some things in regard to which I am not quite satisfied with you. I believe you to be a brave and skilful soldier, which of course I like. I also believe that you do not mix politics with your profession, in which you are right. You have confidence in yourself, which is a valuable, if not indispensable quality. You are ambitious, which, within reasonable bounds, does good rather than harm ; but I think that during General Burnside's command of the army you have taken counsel of your ambition and thwarted him as much as you could, in which you did a great wrong to the country and to a most meritorious and honourable brother officer. I have heard, in such a way as to believe it, of your recently saying that both the Army and the Government needed a dictator. Of course it was not for this, but in spite of it, that I gave you the command. Only those Generals who gain successes can set up as dictators. What I now ask of you is a military success, and I will risk the dictatorship. The Government will support you to the utmost of its ability, which is neither more nor less than it has done and will do for all commanders. I much fear that the spirit which you have aided to infuse into the army of criticising their commander and

withholding confidence from him will now turn upon you.
Neither you nor Napoleon, if he were alive again, could get any
good out of an army while such a spirit prevails in it; and now
beware of rashness.   Beware of rashness, but with energy and
sleepless vigilance go forward and give us victories.'

Hooker took this letter to heart and set about his
first task—to restore the morale and discipline of his
army.   This was done in a wonderfully short time, but
it was necessary to wait till the latter end of April
before the roads were fit for big operations.   Fredericksburg had been a straightforward frontal attack; Chancellorsville consisted of nine days of wide manœuvres.

Lee still lay in the position south of the Rappahannock.   His own wish was to resume the offensive and
invade Maryland, as he did later on in the year; for
this, however, he was not strong enough, because
Longstreet, with two of his divisions, had been taken
away by order of President Davis for operations in Carolina.   Lee, therefore, contented himself with improving
his position, throwing out cavalry and detachments to
watch the river on his flanks.

The opening move was left to Hooker.   Any further
attempt at a frontal attack was out of the question,
and therefore the Federals must cross the river by
manœuvre.   Hooker's superior numbers, 130,000 to
60,000, gave him the power to threaten several points
before developing his main advance.

After sending his cavalry under Stoneman on a fruitless mission towards the west, Hooker started his main
attempt on 27th April.   Sedgwick with two Corps was
sent to cross below Fredericksburg and to make a
demonstration to hold the Confederates in their lines.
Hooker himself with the 5th, 11th, and 12th Corps
marched twenty-six miles up the Rappahannock and
crossed it, then turned southwards to cross the Rapidan
at Germanna and Ely's fords, and then eastwards to
Chancellorsville.   To connect the two wings the 3rd

JOSEPH HOOKER (1814–1879)
Major General, U.S.A.

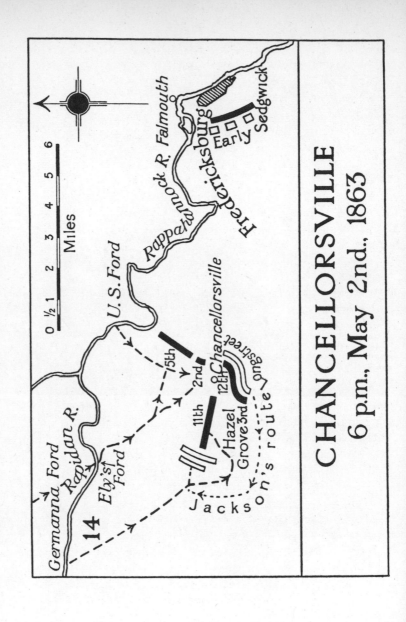

CHANCELLORSVILLE
6 p.m., May 2nd., 1863

14

Corps was left at Falmouth and the 2nd opposite the U.S. Ford. (See Sketch 14.)

By the evening of the 30th the turning movement had been successfully carried out. Three corps were already concentrated about Chancellorsville, the 2nd was crossing the U.S. Ford which had been abandoned by the enemy, the 3rd had been ordered up from Falmouth.

It was not till the evening of the 29th that Lee got full reports from Stuart's cavalry. Jackson was anxious to attack Sedgwick's force which was close at hand and could scarcely be supported by the Federals. Lee, however, judged correctly that Sedgwick's move was only a feint, so he left 10,000 under Early to watch it and turned his serious attention to Hooker's main body.

May 1st. Sedgwick (40,000) was facing Early (10,000) at Fredericksburg. Hooker (70,000) was at Chancellorsville, Lee and Jackson (50,000) marching towards Hooker. Fredericksburg to Chancellorsville 12 miles.

At midday Hooker moved eastwards and met Jackson. There was a dense fog which upset the signalling arrangements and the advance was through a forest with thick undergrowth. Uncertain of the situation, Hooker decided to draw back and take up a position at Chancellorsville; a strong line of breastworks was built, facing east, with its left on the Rappahannock, its right near Hazel Grove. It was held by four corps; the 11th Corps lay a couple of miles to the west of Chancellorsville. Sedgwick had been ordered to send one of his corps to join the main body by way of the U.S. Ford.

As Hooker fell back to this position, the Confederates pressed strongly after him, and by sunset were facing his powerful line of breastworks.

Hooker's retreat on this day has been severely blamed; it was the first symptom of the hesitation which afterwards ended fatally. He had outflanked Lee in the opening move and forced him to abandon the formidable position at Fredericksburg : he had concentrated 70,000 men on the enemy's flank, threatening their rear. But at this moment he gave up the initiative and adopted a passive attitude. It was now Lee's turn to take the offensive and outflank Hooker.

May 2nd. Jackson's staff, infected with the energy of their leader, had spent their time searching for roads through the densely timbered woods. Early in the morning one of them brought in the information about a road leading round the south of the Federal line, and in a few minutes Lee and Jackson had settled on their plan. Once more Lee dared to separate the two wings of his small force in the very face of a more numerous foe, and, as at Second Bull Run, Jackson was to undertake the adventurous part.

At 4 a.m. Jackson with 30,000 started on his march. He had some fifteen miles to go, on a single road, and it took him over twelve hours to complete the semicircle. He then formed up for attack, facing east.

The early stage of his move was observed by the Federals, but at that time he was heading south-west, and Hooker took it as an indication that Lee was going to retire. The 3rd Corps was dispatched southwards to harass the retreat but failed to get in front of Jackson, and after he had swung round to the north-west they seem to have lost sight of him entirely. Howard, who commanded the 11th Corps, was quite unconscious of the storm that was about to burst upon him, and there were no precautions taken against any movement from the west.

At 6 p.m. Jackson gave the order to attack. The 11th Corps, taken by surprise, was thrown into confusion and swept away. The Confederates followed furiously and by 7 p.m. were within a mile and a half

of Hooker's head-quarters at Chancellorsville. Here
the Federals had collected some detachments to make a
stand, and a very gallant charge by a small handful of
cavalry gave them a respite which, though brief, was of
infinite value.

About 8 p.m. Jackson learned that his leading troops
had come to a halt and were in much confusion. With
his staff he rode up to urge them forward, and got in
between them and the Federal skirmishers, who opened
fire on the little party. As they retired through the
wood in the gathering dusk, they were mistaken by
their own men for a body of the enemy's cavalry. A
volley was fired—and Jackson fell, mortally wounded.

It can scarcely be doubted that the loss of this one
man made all the difference to the further progress of
the battle. Jackson would certainly not have rested
until his thrust had been pushed right home, but no
one knew exactly what his intentions had been and no
one was on the spot to assume the command. It is one
of the drawbacks of a ' one man show ' that the one
man is indispensable to its success. So it was in this
case ; the Confederate advance got no farther and the
Unionists were given a chance to pull themselves together.

May 3rd. Jackson's brilliant move had caused consternation at times amounting to panic in the Federal
head-quarters, but in spite of this Hooker's situation
was far from bad if he had taken advantage of it. He
still had 70,000 men on the spot : three corps close
round Chancellorsville, three more a couple of miles to
the north ; with the exception of the 11th Corps none
of them had been beaten and half of them had scarcely
been engaged. He knew that the enemy was divided
into two wings which lay east and west of him. Even
united they could not equal him in numbers; separately
either of them must be much inferior. Most probably

the thick wood prevented any close connexion between them. So far from his position being hopeless it was the ideal one for which Napoleon had always striven— a central position with fresh troops close at hand, between the enemy's widely separated wings.

It has been said by many authors that Lee out-generaled Hooker ; surely it would be more correct to say he ' out-nerved ' him. Lincoln, in his last interview with Hooker, had said : ' In your next battle *put in all your men.*' Had this wise advice been carried out, the Federals were in a winning position. But it was Lee, and not Hooker, who acted on Lincoln's advice : though he began by breaking an elementary rule of tactics, in dividing his forces while in touch with the enemy, he had the nerve to throw in every man— and so came out triumphant.

On May 1st the bold attitude of the Confederates had made Hooker hesitate and draw back : on the 2nd their still bolder attitude had left him bewildered : on the 3rd his only thought was to keep open his road to the fords and make good his escape. It has been pleaded as an excuse for him that he was stunned by a shell which hit a pillar against which he was leaning, but this did not happen before 9 a.m. and by that time it was clear that the Unionist army was not going to make any offensive movement.

The Confederates attacking from both sides got possession of Chancellorsville by midday, and thus effected junction between their two wings. Instead of calling up his fresh corps, Hooker fell back northwards to join them and took a position facing south to cover the fords of the Rappahannock. On the night of the 6th he crossed the whole of his force back to the north bank.

After taking Chancellorsville, Lee did not press his attack, but turned round on Sedgwick. This General had taken Marye's Hill, above Fredericksburg, on the

3rd, and might have assisted Hooker very much if the latter had kept Lee busy. On the 4th, however, he found that Early had been strongly reinforced by Lee, and that Hooker was doing nothing. After making some resistance, he withdrew to the north bank.

The Federals' losses amounted to over 16,000. The Confederates lost 12,000—and Stonewall Jackson.

XVI

GETTYSBURG

ONCE more the two armies faced each other with the broad stream of the Rappahannock between them. This time it was Lee who made the big move. Though Longstreet, who had been away in Northern Carolina with two of his divisions, was now on his way back, he would only bring the Confederates' numbers up to 70,000, and this was quite insufficient for a direct attack on Hooker. Another advance into Maryland, though it would leave open the road to Richmond, seemed to Lee the only hope of gaining a decisive success. Such a success was now very necessary to the South ; as long as there had been prospects of foreign intervention, President Davis had preferred a defensive attitude ; but though these prospects were kept alive by some injudicious speeches in England, they took no material shape. During the month of May Grant's pressure on Vicksburg had roused alarm in the South, and made the situation much more acute. Lee had no illusions. 'We should not conceal from ourselves,' he wrote, 'that our resources in men are constantly diminishing and the disproportion in this respect between us and our enemies is constantly augmenting.' The advantages to be gained by an invasion of the North were considerable :

1. It would probably force Hooker to evacuate Virginia.
2. It would enable the Confederates to replenish supplies from the enemy's resources.
3. It would spread consternation in the big industrial cities of the North ; would increase the dis-

GEORGE GORDON MEADE (1815–1872)
Major General, U.S.A.

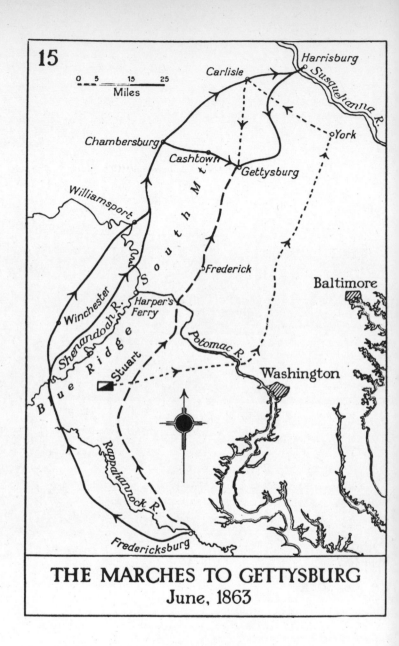

THE MARCHES TO GETTYSBURG
June, 1863

content felt against the Union Government, and give an impetus to the Democratic movement which, already strengthened by the results of Fredericksburg and Chancellorsville, was demanding peace.

4. It might provide an opportunity for the active Confederates to outwit their more numerous but less mobile opponents—in fact, it was the best chance for a decisive victory in the field.

June 1863. Lee gave his troops a month's rest before starting towards the north on June 3rd. His army of 70,000 consisted of three corps, under Longstreet, Ewell, and A. P. Hill, with 9,000 cavalry under Stuart. Ewell led the way, the other two following with big intervals—Lee never had any hesitation about dividing his forces for purposes of manœuvre.

Ewell marched by Culpeper into the Shenandoah Valley (see Sketch 15) ; after meeting with some resistance from the garrison of Winchester (under Milroy) he crossed the Potomac on June 15th. Longstreet followed. Hill had been left to watch Hooker and stood fast about Fredericksburg till June 13th. At one time there was a space of 120 miles between the head and tail of Lee's column.

As soon as the Federals were aware of the enemy's movement to the north-west, Hooker proposed to take the counter offensive and make for Richmond. In reply Lincoln wrote a letter which is a clear statement of his views :

' I have but one idea which I think worth suggesting to you, and that is, in case you find Lee coming to the north of the Rappahannock I would by no means cross to the south of it. If he should leave a rear force at Fredericksburg, tempting you to fall upon it, it would fight in intrenchments and have you at a disadvantage, and so, man for man, worst you at that point, while his main force would in some way be getting an advantage of you northward. In one word, I would not take any risk of being entangled upon the river like an ox jumped half over a fence, and liable to be torn by dogs in front and rear, without a fair chance to gore one way or kick the other.'

A few days later, when Lee's movement had developed :

'If you had Richmond invested to-day you would not be able to take it in twenty days. Meanwhile your communications and with them your army would be ruined. I think Lee's army and not Richmond is your sure objective point. If he comes toward the upper Potomac, follow on his flank and on his inside track, shortening your line as he lengthens his. Fight him too, when opportunity offers. If he stays where he is, fret him and fret him.'

In accordance with this advice, Hooker moved up towards Harper's Ferry, crossed the Potomac on June 25th and was at Frederick City on the 27th.

The invasion had roused the States of the North to strenuous efforts. At Harrisburg, Philadelphia, Pittsburg, and other cities, local authorities enrolled men, raised earthworks, and organized measures for defence, while the journalists provided the Government with much unsolicited advice. One detachment of militia did good work in destroying the Columbia bridge over the Susquehanna—but beyond this they were unable to check Ewell's marauding parties.

On the 28th Lee's main body (Longstreet and Hill) was about Chambersburg. Ewell was at Carlisle and threatening Harrisburg, with one division at York and several smaller parties collecting supplies. But Stuart's cavalry had disappeared.

In the course of the past twelve months Stuart had made several wonderful raids in rear of the Federal lines : first in the Peninsula, again before Second Bull Run, then after Antietam. On each occasion he did some damage to the enemy's communications, collected information and supplies, and had come back unscathed. Such dashing exploits must evoke admiration, and the moral effect of them was great although the material results were small. His successes tempted him to repeat the performance—this time with results that were fatal to his own side.

After some engagements with the Federal cavalry in the neighbourhood of the Blue Ridge, he shook himself free on June 26th and got clean away. He crossed the Potomac between Hooker and Washington; captured a supply train close to the Capital; broke up the Baltimore and Ohio Railway; pushed on to York where he expected to meet Ewell. The latter, however, had already left that town, so Stuart went on to Carlisle which he also found empty. Turning south he succeeded in rejoining Lee on July 2nd—with men and horses utterly worn out. During these momentous six days Lee, who had hitherto been so well informed, was working in the dark.

Hooker Resigns. Up to the 26th the movements of the Federals had been well carried out. But there had been ill feeling for some time between Hooker and Halleck which now came to a head. There was a garrison of 10,000 on the Maryland Height, opposite Harper's Ferry, which Halleck ordered to remain there as a threat to Lee's communications; Hooker wanted this force to join his main body. After some arguments Hooker apparently lost his temper on June 27th, demanded that the dispute be referred to the President, and, without waiting for a reply, followed his telegram up with another offering his resignation. Lincoln accepted it at once.

A change of generals at such a moment was a desperate expedient, and Lincoln himself was well aware of the danger of ' swapping horses while crossing a stream '. But I think his quick decision shows a fine grasp of the possibilities which now presented themselves. The Confederates were no longer in an impregnable position, as at Fredericksburg; they had pushéd fifty miles into the North, leaving a big river and a long line of communications behind them. The Federal army was certainly superior in numbers ; its cavalry was holding its own and bringing in good information which was supplemented by the inhabitants. Though the result of the last two battles had been bad, no fault could be found with the fighting qualities of the troops ; the staff work was improving and the marching was good. There was therefore a better chance than ever before of striking a blow if only the Union Commander would act with resolution and ' put all his men in '. Was Hooker the man to do it ? He had been beaten once by Lee—' out-nerved '—and there were some signs of a recurrence of the malady. No doubt the desire to make a dash at Richmond could be supported by the argument ' attack is the best means of defence ' ; but on the other hand it might be construed as a wish to avoid immediate encounter with his formidable opponent. The petulance displayed in his quarrels with Halleck betrayed excitement which amounted to agitation. Finally, perhaps on the eve of a big battle, he had offered to resign. Such a man could not be feeling any confidence in his power to achieve victory, or surely he would have jumped at the chance to wipe out his late defeat. Lincoln, whose own calm was unruffled even in his most despondent moments, had been watching the symptoms, and when the last outbreak confirmed his suspicions he had no hesitation in making up his mind at once. The same night Meade received orders to take up command.

General G. G. Meade. The new Chief was a Pennsylvanian, forty-seven years old, of good family, and very highly educated. He had commanded a Division at Fredericksburg, where he was one of the few generals who earned renown, also at Chancellorsville. Tall and straight, with an expression that has been described as

JAMES EWELL BROWN ("Jeb") STUART (1833–1864)
Major General, C.S.A.

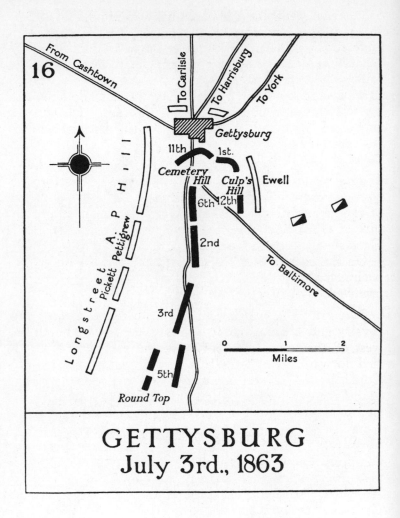

GETTYSBURG
July 3rd., 1863

16

From Cashtown

To Carlisle

To Harrisburg

To York

Gettysburg

11th

1st.

Cemetery
Hill

Culp's
Hill

Ewell

6th

12th

2nd

To Baltimore

Longstreet

Pickett

Pettigrew

A P Hill

3rd

5th

Round Top

0   1   2

Miles

' somewhat saturnine ', reserved but sometimes irritable in manner, with none of the personality which had endeared McClellan to his men, but a thorough and reliable soldier. The victory at Gettysburg, which followed six days after his appointment, silenced any possible criticism which might have been made about his selection and consolidated his position. He continued in command of the Army of the Potomac till the end of the war.

June 30th. Reports had reached Lee that the Federal army was coming up, so he issued orders for a concentration of his scattered forces. By the evening of the 30th Hill was at Cashtown, Longstreet behind him at Chambersburg, Ewell ten miles north-east of Gettysburg.

On the Federal side a cavalry brigade under Buford occupied Gettysburg. The infantry Corps were from twelve to twenty miles south of that point.

July 1st. The first encounter was between Buford's cavalry and a detachment of Hill's on a ridge north-west of the town. On both sides supports were hurried forward. Reynolds brought up the 1st Union Corps, but he himself was killed soon afterwards ; the 11th Corps arrived about noon. Towards 2 p.m. the Confederates began to receive strong reinforcements from Ewell, whose troops were coming in from the north-east. The Unionists, being attacked from both flanks, were obliged to fall back through the town and take up position just south of it on Cemetery Hill. Here they were joined by two more corps, and the Confederates did not press their attack any farther.

Lee had not planned to take the offensive, Hill's movement being intended only as a reconnaissance; but, as the result of the first day's fighting, he found himself committed to a general attack.

July 2nd. The Confederate attack was not launched

until well on in the afternoon.[1] By this time the Federals had all their corps on the ground.

The front line was along a low ridge which ran from Gettysburg to Round Top Hill, 3 miles to the south. The northern flank was curled right back to face Ewell's Corps which was coming from the north-east. This gave the position the shape of a fish-hook.

About 4 p.m. Longstreet attacked the southern end of the position, but beyond driving in some troops which had been posted in front of the main line, he was unable to effect anything before dark.

Farther north two brigades of Hill's Corps reached the crest of the ridge, but being unsupported were forced back. Ewell, who had been ready since sunrise, was ordered not to advance till Longstreet moved. This delayed him so long that it was late when he attacked, and he could gain no ground except at one point, Culp's Hill, from which the Federals had been withdrawn.

July 3rd. Like Lee, Meade had not intended to fight at Gettysburg; he preferred a position twelve miles farther south, on Pipe's Creek. During the night of the 2nd he held a council of war with his Corp Commanders, and as a result of their reports and votes he decided to stand fast.

At daybreak the Unionists made an attack to drive out the enemy who had gained a footing on Culp's Hill. After five hours' struggle the Confederates were forced back, and this ended the fighting at the northern end of the line.

Lee ordered Longstreet to make the main assault with his own Corps and part of Hill's on the Federal centre. As on the previous day Longstreet showed obvious

---

[1] Longstreet has been severely blamed for his slowness on this and the next day. There is no doubt that he was strongly averse to attacking, and it is said that he deliberately postponed the execution of the orders given by Lee. The bitter controversy which has raged on this point is outside the scope of this book.

reluctance, and it was not till 2 p.m. that the attack was launched—and even then it was made by only two divisions, Pickett's and Pettigrew's, about 15,000 men in all. These divisions covered themselves with immortal glory—but their task was an impossible one ; they had to advance across the open for about a mile against the steady and well-posted Unionists. With desperate courage they pressed forward ; Pickett's division lost no less than 3,392 men out of 4,500—including all the commanders of brigades and regiments. A handful of them broke into the Federal front line and laid hands upon the guns—but no supports were available, and a counter-attack drove them back. Lee's great effort had failed and the battle was over.

In the three days the Federals lost 23,000 out of 93,000 ; the Confederates 20,000 (some writers put it as high as 30,000) out of 70,000.

Meade has been censured for not making a general counter-attack to complete the victory. But his own troops had all been heavily engaged and he knew that part of Longstreet's Corps was still intact. Rhodes says :

'It is true that he did not appreciate the magnitude of his victory, but ought the critic to demand from him any greater military sagacity than from Lee ? The Confederate general under similar circumstances did not comprehend how badly he had beaten Burnside at Fredericksburg and did not follow up his success.'

Lee made no attempt to put blame on other shoulders. His nerve did not fail him as he calmly rode up to rally his broken troops. 'General,' he said to one angry brigadier, 'all this has been my fault—it is I that have lost this fight and you must help me out of it the best way you can.'

The Confederate Retreat. On the night of July 4th, amid heavy rain, the defeated army began to retire, and reached the Potomac at Williamsport on the 11th. The

river was in flood and Lee was obliged to take up a
position, expecting to be attacked, until the night of
the 13th, when a bridge was completed and the Confederates escaped to the south bank.

On the day after Gettysburg the Southern fortress of
Vicksburg surrendered to General Grant, as will be
described in a later chapter. The Union States received the news with deep but sober joy, and it was
realized that these two great events marked the
turning point of the war.

Lincoln's Distress. This essay is concerned with
Lincoln's personal part in the war and the brief narrative of events is only intended to provide a standpoint
from which his work can be reviewed. At this time,
during the days following Gettysburg, his attitude provides us with the most signal of all the proofs of his
genius.

It might be imagined that the President, of all men,
would be overjoyed with the news of victory. It was
an undeniable and glorious victory, on a big scale,
wiping out at one blow the disappointments of the
Peninsula, Bull Run, Fredericksburg, and Chancellorsville. The danger that had so closely menaced the
cities of the North was now averted : the reputation of
Lee and his army for invincibility was shattered : the
fighting power of the Union army was proved and its
moral ascendancy established. The political gains were
enormous : it justified the action of the Government
and strengthened its position. It silenced the croaking
of the ravens who had been demanding peace at any
price. It was a snub to the prophets at home and
abroad who had been declaring the cause of the Union
to be hopeless.

Such thoughts might well have filled the President's
mind to the exclusion of all others—at least in the first
intoxication of victory. Yet, so far from this being the

case, Lincoln's mind was filled with nothing but disappointment. He penned to the victor words far harsher than he had ever addressed to McClellan, Pope, Burnside, or Hooker—and in them we see how truly he judged past events, how clearly he foresaw events to come. From the past he judged the stubborn pride of the South, the brilliance of Lee, the valour of the Confederate soldiers, and he saw that though the Union had won a battle it had not yet won the war. He saw how Lee would again fall back behind the rivers and forests and mud of Virginia, he saw the struggle and sacrifice of blood that would be entailed in crushing that wonderful army. His forecast filled him with horror and dismay.

And here, in the early days of July, Lee's army was within easy reach. Meade had 60,000 veterans flushed with victory and 20,000 fresh men had joined him. Lee could scarcely have more than 40,000, suffering from a heavy defeat ; his road was blocked by an unfordable river ; he must stand to fight. As Lincoln himself had said ; ' Lee's army and not Richmond is your sure objective point.' The capture of that army might well finish the war.

This thought seems to have flashed into Lincoln's mind from the first and was not prompted by any one else. He spent some time on July 6th at the telegraph office listening to Meade's reports, and on his return home at 7 p.m. he sat down and wrote to Halleck. ' I left the telegraph office a good deal dissatisfied. You know I did not like Meade's phrase : " Drive the invaders from our soil ! " ' A clear indication of the main idea of his strategy—*not to drive away the enemy but to prevent him getting away.*

Next day he wrote—' We have certain information that Vicksburg surrendered to General Grant on the 4th of July. Now, if General Meade can complete his work, so gloriously prosecuted thus far, by the literal or substantial destruction of Lee's army the rebellion will be over.'

Throughout the following days he was torn with anxiety. About noon on the 14th news came in that Lee had escaped. Rhodes says : ' Lincoln could hardly restrain his irritation within bounds. On the spur of the moment he gave vent to his feelings in a letter to Meade which on second thoughts he did not sign or send.'

The letter was as follows :

' I am sorry to be the author of the slightest pain to you. You fought and beat the enemy at Gettysburg, and of course, to say the least, his loss was as great as yours. He retreated, and you did not, it seems to me, pressingly pursue him. You had at least 20,000 veteran troops with you and as many more raw ones within supporting distance, all in addition to those who fought with you at Gettysburg ; while it was not possible that he had received a single recruit, and yet you stood and let the river run down, bridges be built, and the enemy move away at his leisure without attacking him. Again, my dear General, I do not believe you appreciate the magnitude of the disaster involved in Lee's escape. He was within your easy grasp, and to have closed upon him would, in connexion with our other successes, have ended the war. As it is the war will be prolonged indefinitely. If you could not safely attack Lee last Monday, how can you possibly do so south of the river, when you can take with you very few more than two-thirds of the force you then had in hand ? It would seem unreasonable to expect, and I do not expect, that you can now effect much. Your golden opportunity is gone, and I am distressed immeasurably because of it.'

But Lee had escaped. The letter would have rendered Meade's position intolerable—in fact would have amounted to dismissing him, which would look like ingratitude to the soldiers who had fought so hard at Gettysburg. It is all very well to shoot a general after a failure, *pour encourager les autres*, but to do so after a victory would not have a steadying effect on the nerves of his successor. So Lincoln let the sun go down on his wrath and faced the gloomy future with grim courage.

It would be too much to say that certain victory was within Meade's reach, for there is no such thing as certainty in war—but it is a fact that he had a better chance than ever presented itself to the Unionists, either before or afterwards. It is easy for us to see this now, in the light of history. Lincoln, the amateur strategist, grasped it at the time, while his professional soldiers were congratulating themselves on ' driving the invader from our soil '.

XVII

THE WEST

THE war in the East was confined to a narrow area. In the West it ranged down the Mississippi from Cairo to Vicksburg, all over the States of Kentucky and Tennessee, through Georgia to the coast ; besides this there were minor operations lower down the Mississippi and on its west bank. On each side the forces were divided into two or more armies which were constantly being given new names, new commanders, and new objectives, with the result that the narrative jumps from one place to another in a confusing manner. Details are certainly intricate, but there is little difficulty in understanding the general course of operations if a beginning be made with a rough outline on the map—as indeed should always be done in the study of Military History. The operations fall under three broad headings : A, the conquest of the River Mississippi ; B, the occupation of Chattanooga ; C, the advance from Chattanooga through Georgia to the coast.

The Mississippi. There were three important lines which mark the stages of the Federal advance :

1. A line from Columbus (on the river) through Forts Henry and Donelson to Nashville, the capital of Tennessee. This line was secured as the result of Grant's operations in February '62.

2. A line from Memphis (on the river) to Corinth. This was reached in June '62, chiefly as the result of a successful battle fought by Grant at

172

HENRY WAGER HALLECK (1815–1872)
Major General, U.S.A.

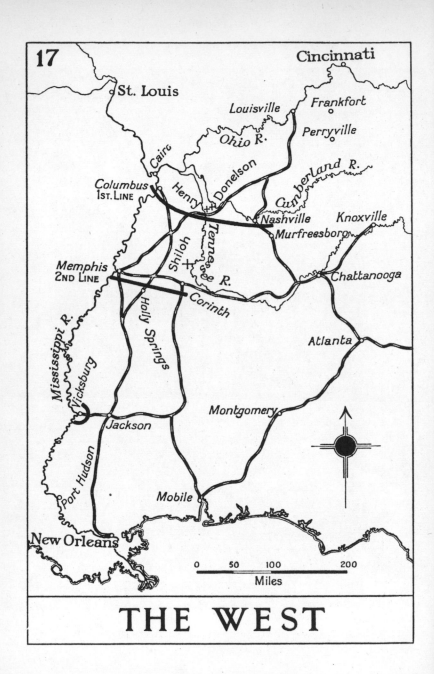

THE WEST

Shiloh, twenty miles north of Corinth, on April 6th and 7th.

During the autumn of '62 a diversion occurred. The Southerners, under Bragg, starting from Chattanooga, made a raid northwards right through Tennessee and Kentucky nearly as far as Louisville. There the Federals, under Buell, collected superior forces, and Bragg was obliged to fall back after a sharp engagement at Perryville. Bragg made a second effort towards Nashville in December but was repulsed at Murfreesboro (Stone's River). This brought to an end the operations of the winter of '62–'63.

3. The capture of Vicksburg. This was effected on July 4th, '63, by the dogged perseverance of Grant, after several failures. As a result the Mississippi was opened up throughout its length to the U.S. gunboats, and the Confederacy was converted into a sort of island.

Speaking broadly the criticism may be made that both sides were attending too much to the occupation of territory instead of aiming at the destruction of the enemy's forces. This, however, is not surprising : Kentucky wanted to remain neutral : in Tennessee the western half was strongly inclined to the South, while the eastern half, a mountainous district, was equally inclined to the North : both States were likely to be swayed by the side which occupied them. In addition to this the forces were not very unequal, and in such a wide area it was difficult to drive the enemy into a corner ; therefore there was little opportunity of inflicting a decisive blow. In the battles in the open we see one side forced off the field, but the casualties were fairly evenly divided. The Confederates lost many men through clinging to strategic points and locking up garrisons in them—at Donelson 12,000

surrendered, at Vicksburg 30,000, and some 10,000 at
other forts on the river. This was bad strategy when
they were in sore need of men.

Lincoln and the West. As might be expected there is
much less trace of Lincoln's personal touch in the West
than in the East. He was far removed from the scene,
and had no acquaintance with the leading actors. He
watched events with close attention and sometimes
with impatience, but there were no moments of tense
excitement such as were caused by Lee's invasions of
the North, no cases where the President felt called
upon to upset the plans of his generals. In fact his
part may be summed up in a few words—he sought
for a man to take command and when he found one he
left him alone. Needless to say that man was Ulysses
Grant.

General U. S. Grant. If, at the outset of the war,
any one had been asked to hazard a guess at the name
of the man who would be Commander-in-Chief at the
end of it, the probability is that Grant would have
been the last person to get a vote.

He was born in Ohio in 1822, and spent his early
days on his father's farm. He was sent to school very
regularly but admits that he was ' not studious in
habit '. Through the political influence of a friend
a cadetship was obtained at West Point where he spent
four wearisome years and graduated in the lower half
of his class. ' A military life had no charms for me
and I had not the faintest idea of staying in the army.' [1]
Shortly after he got his first commission he went
through the Mexican War and gained promotion for
gallantry in the field. During most of this time he
was Quartermaster of his regiment, and therefore in
charge of the transport ; the experience was of real
value to him later on, when so much depended upon

[1] *Memoirs of U. S. Grant*, p. 38.

the marching powers of his troops. In 1854 he threw up his commission, and it seems sadly true that had he not done so he would have been dismissed on account of his drinking habits. During the next few years he was on the downward grade till, at the outbreak of the war, he was completely down and out. If there was any ambition in him there was not the capacity or will to pursue it. At times he took a small part in the leather business of his father, but evidently was not a business man. He lived for the most part on his debts.

When the war began he applied to Washington for employment, also to McClellan, an old acquaintance. In the end he got a comparatively humble appointment as colonel of a Volunteer Regiment—and it does not seem that he expected anything better.

From this he worked his way up to be Lieutenant-General of the U.S. Army, and every step was earned by his own endeavour. There was no political influence at his back, no recognized position such as Lee and McClellan held before the war. He was not a student of military science, nor a man of military appearance and habits. The senior officers knew him and distrusted him. Up to the very moment of his success at Vicksburg his position was precarious and he would have been removed had it not been for Lincoln's faith.

The Opening Situation. From the outset General Winfield Scott had seen the importance of the Mississippi and had suggested that a defensive attitude should be observed around Washington while the main effort was made in the West. But public opinion in the North could not be reconciled to a plan which foreshadowed a long-drawn-out struggle, and when the Confederacy established its new Capital only a hundred miles from Washington it seemed to challenge a decision in that field. As soon as McClellan got command

his interests were absorbed by the prospects immediately in front of him, and so the operations in the
West, though important, were regarded as subsidiary
to the main advance on Richmond.

Whether it would have been better to concentrate
on one side or the other can now be only a matter of
conjecture.   Concentration for attack is a sound
military principle—but we must look at it both ways ;
had the Federals concentrated to attack Richmond
the Confederates would have concentrated to oppose
them.   The Northern troops in the West detained
a corresponding number of Southern troops, and at the
same time saved the border States, to some extent,
from being overrun or raided.   The States of Illinois,
Indiana, Ohio enrolled large numbers for the Union,
but would have complained bitterly if called on to
send them all to the East, and this had a great deal to
do with the decision to leave two armies west of the
Alleghanies.   These were situated in November 1861
as follows :

1. The Army of the Ohio, under Buell. Based on
   Louisville and facing south towards Nashville.
2. The Army of the Mississippi. It was commanded
   by Halleck, who made his head-quarters in
   St. Louis to deal with the local disturbances.
   The troops were spread over a wide area, but
   the main body was about Cairo under Grant.

In addition to the land forces the Federals had
formed a fleet of gunboats on the river which were
much superior to anything the enemy could put afloat.

To block the big navigable rivers to these gunboats
the Confederates had built several forts on the Mississippi below Cairo, also Fort Henry on the Tennessee
and Fort Donelson on the Cumberland.   The Southern
field army was under A. S. Johnston, covering Nashville and facing Buell.   A detachment under Kirby
Smith was at Knoxville in Eastern Tennessee.

The opening situation provides a pretty example of a strategical problem and how not to solve it.

Lincoln, from the point of view of a politician, had his eye fixed on Knoxville. The people of that district were Unionists, and he was anxious to show that the Union could and would protect those who clung to it. There was a hope that the Federals might find recruits there. Altogether a very laudable desire on the part of the President, so long as it did not clash with military plans.

McClellan also wanted Buell to move on to Knoxville. He was preparing for the main advance in Virginia and wanted the subsidiary movement to assist him. A Federal army at Knoxville would threaten the rear of Virginia and might oblige the Confederates to send a detachment in that direction, thereby depleting their main body. This was quite sound strategy. McClellan therefore urged Buell to march direct from Louisville on Knoxville.

The objection came from Buell. He recognized the importance of Knoxville, but disagreed about the best way of getting there. From Louisville to Knoxville is over two hundred miles : there was no railway : the country roads were very bad, especially in winter, and in some places led across mountains : there were few towns in which supplies could be obtained, and anything like forcible requisitioning would create a bad impression on the ' friendly neutrals ' : the long line of communications would be open to raids by the Confederates, who were very active. In fact the local difficulties were immense. Buell saw the necessity of defeating Johnston before attempting the mere occupation of territory ; he also saw the value of the great rivers Cumberland and Tennessee as lines of supply. He therefore proposed that Halleck should move up the Cumberland while he himself marched on Nashville, making this their first objective. This would force Johnston to fight or to evacuate the whole of Kentucky and part of Tennessee. Later on the movement could be extended towards Knoxville.

Halleck was full of his affairs in Missouri, and his only contribution to the discussion was that Buell's army should be put under his command, though it is not clear what use he proposed to make of it. The idea of a single command, instead of two independent ones, was quite sound and it was eventually adopted.

Ropes argues strongly that Buell was right : Lincoln could only see the political object : McClellan was quite incapable of understanding any difficulties but his own : while Buell was a very efficient soldier, a stern martinet, who could see difficulties without exaggerating them.

While the matter was still being argued McClellan fell ill, in December 1861. Halleck and Buell were told to correspond directly with each other, but neither could give orders. Buell sent one division under Thomas towards Knoxville : about half-way there he had a successful little fight at Mill Springs on January 19th, '62.

Halleck had hitherto done nothing. He declared that 60,000 men were required for the movement up the rivers and he could not spare more than 10,000. But suddenly he changed his mind. It is not clear why he did so—perhaps the success of Thomas spurred him to do something, perhaps he was convinced by the reports from Grant and Commodore Foote, who commanded the fleet. At all events, on February 1st, Grant got orders to move, with 15,000 men and the support of the gunboats.

Fort Henry. This work was badly placed in a low-lying site. As Grant approached, the Confederate Commander decided to move his infantry to Fort Donelson, leaving only a few gunners to delay the

enemy. After a short bombardment on February 6th
the fort was surrendered. Johnston immediately fell
back from Buell's front to Nashville, and foolishly sent
12,000 men to reinforce the garrison of Fort Donelson.

Fort Donelson. Grant had to wait while the flotilla
went down the Tennessee and came up the Cumberland
to assist against Fort Donelson. Then on the 12th he
set out. The gunboats, after a brisk action on the
14th, were forced to retire down the stream, consider-
ably damaged. While Grant was on board one of
them, consulting with Foote, the Confederates made a
sally to cut their way out to Nashville ; they had
cleared a road for themselves and could have escaped,
when through some mistake they were recalled to the
fort. Grant arrived on the scene and took the situation
in hand ; he brought troops up to block the road and
ordered an assault, which took an important part of
the defences by storm. On the 16th Fort Donelson
was surrendered with 12,000 of its garrison.

Halleck had not asked for approval of his plan from
Washington, nor had he asked Buell to co-operate.
But the success of it forced the hand of McClellan,
who had to give up the idea of Knoxville for the time
being. Buell was now ordered on Nashville and
occupied that town without resistance on February
24th. Johnston slipped away to the south.

On March 11th Halleck was given the complete
control in the West, for which he had been clamouring.
This brought Buell under his orders. It is generally
agreed that Buell was the better man and that Lincoln
made a mistake in this appointment. But it was
Halleck's army which had achieved the success.

The first stage in the Federal advance was now
complete and Halleck decided to push on towards
Corinth. Grant moved up the Tennessee and camped
his army on the west bank at Pittsburg Landing near

Shiloh Church; he had 45,000 men. Buell with 37,000 was ordered from Nashville to join him.

Shiloh, April 6th and 7th. Johnston had collected at Corinth about 40,000, including some garrisons from abandoned posts. He saw a chance of attacking Grant before Buell arrived. This led to the Battle of Shiloh, sometimes known as Pittsburg Landing.

Grant was caught napping. His camp was very badly arranged for defence, without entrenchments or a regular outpost line. Practically no patrolling was done to the front. Worst of all, when the Confederates made their surprise attack on April 6th, Grant himself was nine miles in rear on the other bank of the river. Most of the battle-field was covered with wood which caused much confusion in the fighting. During the first day the Federals were thrown back in much disorder and were nearly forced into the river.

Halleck had not impressed upon Buell that there was any urgency, and the latter was moving by fairly easy stages on his way to join Grant. His troops began to arrive on the 6th and some of them were hurried across the river to help the hard-pressed Federals on the west bank. Grant, however, has maintained that his own army held up the Confederate advance and had no need of supports. During the night the remainder of Buell's army was brought on to the field, and Grant, thus reinforced, ordered a general advance at daylight on the 7th.

Johnston had been killed on the 6th and Beauregard took command. The Confederates were forced back but retired in good order. Grant did not press the pursuit.

The Federals' casualties were 13,000. Beauregard reported a total loss of 10,699, but Grant argues, in his account, that this is much understated.

The Battle of Shiloh and the part taken in it by the

leaders on both sides has raised bitter disputes ; without entering into them it may be said that Grant was not at his best either in his arrangements beforehand or in his pursuit afterwards.

Halleck arrived to take command in person on April 11th and began a very cautious advance towards Corinth, which he found evacuated on June 2nd. This move forced the Confederates to abandon Memphis—and the second stage in the Federal advance was complete. Pope had meanwhile been working down the Mississippi with much success ; he picked up 7,000 prisoners on his way. When he joined Halleck with his 10,000 men the Federal forces at Corinth amounted to 100,000.

July 1862. McClellan's campaign in the Peninsula had come to an end with the Seven Days. The President felt the need of a responsible military adviser by his side ; the Federals in the West had been advancing, surely if slowly, and Halleck had got, or had taken, the credit—and therefore when it became necessary to find a successor to McClellan the choice naturally fell on Halleck. But before he went to Washington he had sketched out a plan of campaign and issued orders which affected the course of operations during the next six months.

His main idea was to revert to the project of occupying East Tennessee, and Chattanooga was obviously the key to the whole situation. Grant was therefore ordered to remain about Corinth while Buell marched on Chattanooga, which lies one hundred and fifty miles to the eastward. Halleck made a serious mistake, however, in ordering Buell to move along the railroad which runs direct to his objective ; it was exposed to raids from the Confederate cavalry, who showed brilliant daring under the celebrated leaders Forrest and Morgan. Buell saw the danger and asked to be allowed to make his advance from Nashville, thus covering his line of communications, but more than a month was wasted before he succeeded in getting Halleck to agree.

Bragg's Offensive. The Confederates had not failed to make the most of the respite given them by Halleck's slowness, and divined that Chattanooga would be the next point to be attacked. Beauregard had resigned owing to ill health : Bragg succeeded him, and by the beginning of August collected his forces at Chattanooga. But he was not content with passive resistance ; Lee, having dealt with McClellan in the Peninsula, was now preparing for his first invasion of the North ; it was clear that if the Confederates could take the offensive in the West at the same time the moral effect would be more than doubled.

The plan was that Kirby Smith should move northwest from Knoxville and join Bragg, who marched due north from Chattanooga. Buell, who was at Nashville, now had to race to get to Louisville before the enemy ; he would not have succeeded had Bragg kept straight on, but the latter, after getting the best of the start, suddenly turned off to the eastward and joined Kirby Smith at Frankfort, the Capital of Kentucky. He held the extraordinary view that he must signalize his entry into the State by installing a Secessionist Government in its Capital.

This gave Buell time to reach Louisville on September 25th, and he found the town in a state of alarm. The Governors of Indiana and Ohio were busy enrolling troops for their own protection. Reinforced by some of these Buell had 58,000, and on October 1st he advanced against the enemy. The Confederates began to fall back. An accidental encounter at Perryville on October 7th developed into a battle which was fiercely contested but indecisive in result. Bragg, seeing that

he was outnumbered and that Kentucky did not
respond to his call for recruits, decided to abandon that
State and its new Governor to the Federals. Buell
followed him, but finding that the Confederates would
not stand to fight, he returned to Nashville. There on
October 30th he received orders to hand over command
to Rosecrans.

Buell was an unlucky man. Though a good organizer
he had none of the personal charm which made
McClellan so popular with the troops, and he had
incurred the dislike of the Governors of Indiana, Ohio,
and Illinois. His failure to block Bragg's advance, to
bring him to battle, and to press the pursuit, was
painted in the worst colours—and, naturally but un-
justly, it seemed to be like McClellan's conduct after
Antietam. In the background was his old objection
to marching on Knoxville in December '61 ; when, in
August '62. Kirby Smith made this same march the
reverse way it seemed to Lincoln that Buell's objection
had been ill-founded ; the difference between marching in December and in August had not yet been
realized. Halleck tried to save his former colleague,
but Halleck's failure to grasp the situation in Washington, after Second Bull Run, had shaken Lincoln's faith
in his judgement. On October 31st Governor Morton
of Indiana telegraphed to the President—' Bragg has
escaped with his army. . . . The butchery of our troops
at Perryville was terrible, and resulted from a large
portion of the enemy being precipitated on a small
portion of ours. Sufficient time was thus gained by the
enemy to enable them to escape. . . . In the North-
West distrust and despair are seizing upon the hearts
of the people.' Morton was supported by the
Governors of Ohio and Illinois ; these three were able
' War Governors ' who put the military situation
before party politics ; they were personally acquainted
with Buell, and there is little doubt that Lincoln's

decision was based on their judgement. Buell was unlucky, but, as Rhodes says, ' little wonder that the President gave the word for his removal.'

Corinth, October 14th. While Bragg was in Kentucky the Confederates had been busy against Grant, to prevent him from reinforcing Buell. Two battles were fought, at Iuka on September 19th and at Corinth on October 14th. On both occasions Rosecrans was in immediate command of the Unionists and gained successes which earned for him promotion to take the place of Buell.

Rosecrans, like his predecessor, was urged to advance into East Tennessee. He insisted, however, on repairing his railways and collecting a reserve of supplies at Nashville. On December 26th he began his move towards Chattanooga and found Bragg's army facing him at Murfreesboro, thirty miles south of Nashville.

Murfreesboro (Stone's River), 31st December 1862. The battle began on December 31st and lasted for three days. Each commander planned to make an attack on the right flank of the enemy ; this caused much shuffling of the troops as they were called to support an attack at one point or repel an attack at another. Each side could claim temporary successes but there was no decisive movement. On January 2nd Bragg withdrew his worn-out forces and left the field to Rosecrans, who, however, was not in a state to pursue. Both sides went into winter quarters, the Confederates covering Chattanooga, the Federals round Nashville, and nothing further was done in this area during the next six months.

XVIII

GRANT IN THE WEST

Lincoln and Grant.

I HAVE never been able to get away from a suspicion that it was the bad report circulated about Grant which first attracted Lincoln's sympathy towards him. We cannot know all that was said, but some idea of the colour of it may be seen in the following dispatches :

Halleck to McClellan, 2nd March 1862 (a fortnight after the taking of Fort Donelson) :

' I have had no communication with General Grant for over a week. He left his command without my authority and went to Nashville. It is hard to censure a successful general immediately after a victory but I think he richly deserves it. I can get no returns, no reports, no information of any kind from him. Satisfied with his victory he sits down and enjoys it without any regard for the future.'

McClellan to Halleck, March 3rd :

' Your despatch of last evening received. The success of our cause demands that proceedings such as Grant's should be at once checked. Do not hesitate to arrest him at once if the good of the service requires it, and place C. F. Smith in command. You are at liberty to regard this as a positive order if it will smooth your way.'

Halleck to McClellan, March 4th :

' A rumor has just reached me that Grant has resumed his former bad habits. If so it will account for his repeated neglect of my oft repeated orders. I do not deem it advisable to arrest him at present. . . .'

Halleck to Grant, March 6th :

' General McClellan directs that you report to me daily the number and position of the forces under your command. Your neglect of repeated orders has created great dissatisfaction and seriously interfered with military plans. Your going to Nashville without authority was a matter of serious complaint at Washington, so much so that I was advised to arrest you on your return. ...'

On March 15th, however, Halleck wrote to McClellan that no further action was necessary as Grant had explained that he had been to Nashville to consult with Buell.

Now there can be no doubt that Grant was careless about correspondence, and this is very annoying to a superior. A modern army is almost as dependent on supplies and transport as a warship is on fuel and engines. The Quartermaster, who has to provide rations, ammunition, hospital stores, and transport, can only base his calculations on the returns from the field. No doubt it is trying for a general to sit down after a battle and worry out a lot of figures, but if he neglects to give information, he has no right to complain afterwards when necessary stores are not forthcoming. If Grant had too much to do he ought to have detailed a staff officer to attend to the returns ; in a modern staff there is a special branch responsible for such work. Halleck, who no doubt wanted to help his subordinate, was very naturally annoyed at not knowing where Grant was to be found and at getting no news for a week.

On the other hand, Lincoln, who was far from methodical in his own correspondence, would see only the broad fact that Grant had gained the first solid success which had fallen to the lot of the Union. Complaints about office routine, which no doubt were handed on in some form or other, would seem petty, and perhaps even inspired by jealousy. He was so free from personal jealousy himself that any sign of it inclined his sympathy towards the victim.

McClellan was never remiss in correspondence— quite the reverse—but his famous return about the garrison of Washington prejudiced Lincoln against paper figures. It must have been a relief to turn from the facile scribe to a man like Grant, who wrote neither plans nor complaints but just went and did things. Then there was the rumour about ' bad habits '. Perhaps Halleck was the first to pass it on to Washington, but later on it became many-tongued. A prominent journalist wrote to Chase accusing Grant of gross misconduct, and demanding ' in the name of the Western people and of the Western troops ' that his command should be taken from him and given to Rosecrans. Chase solemnly passed on this letter to the President, adding that ' the reports are too common to be safely or even prudently disregarded '. More rumours came from a General McClernand ; this officer had done good work in raising troops in the West and had been given command of an Army Corps ; not content with this his ambition was to command the whole expedition against Vicksburg, and he intrigued to get Grant removed. Newspapers took up the rumour and circulated it openly.

Lincoln was not the man to entrust an army to a drunkard, but he would not accept rumour as a proof of drunkenness. In March 1863 he sent Charles A. Dana to Grant's head-quarters as special commissioner of the War Department. There was no doubt about the special part of this delicate mission—Dana has left a record of it :

' Stanton sent for me to come to Washington. He wanted someone to go to Grant's army, he said, to report daily to him the military proceedings and to give such information as would enable Mr. Lincoln and him to settle their minds as to Grant, about whom at that time there were many doubts and against whom there was some complaint.'

For some time Grant had been on trial and he knew it. Fortunately he was too wise to show resentment.

Fortunately Dana had judgement and discretion. And in a very short time complete confidence was established between the two men. Dana cleared up the question of bad habits, and his opinion has been thoroughly endorsed by historians ; in addition to this his reports on the situation were much more illuminating than the meagre dispatches of the General.

It might be argued that Dana's mission was in itself a proof of suspicion in Lincoln's mind, but this does not follow of necessity ; it might well have been that he thought it only fair to Grant to get a positive refutation of the calumny. He certainly treated the rumours with open contempt. There is his oft-quoted reply to the virtuous zealots who urged him to dismiss such a bad example—' I wish I knew what brand of whisky he drinks. I would send a barrel to all my other generals.' The anecdote is not quite authentic but very characteristic. Lincoln took his own responsibilities in deadly earnest, but sometimes relieved the strain with outbursts which shocked his audience ; he would read aloud to a Cabinet meeting the jests of Artemus Ward, and meet his gloomy advisers with ' little stories '. He seems to have been oppressed with the starched righteousness of some of those who surrounded him. Charnwood says of Chase, ' He was really a good man until he fell in love with his own goodness.' I think Lincoln must have found a spice of malicious pleasure in telling Chase the news of Grant's victories. At all events it must have been a real pleasure to recall the fact that before the news of victory had arrived Grant was given the assurance that he ' has the full confidence of the Government '.

Grant himself has told us : ' With all the pressure brought to bear upon them both President Lincoln and General Halleck stood by me to the end of the campaign.' Halleck had evidently revised his first impressions.

ULYSSES SIMPSON GRANT (1822–1885)
Lieutenant General, U.S.A.

VICKSBURG

The moves on Vicksburg. While Bragg was raiding Kentucky in August and September '62 Grant was forced to remain inactive round Corinth. Halleck, before leaving, had ordered him to send two divisions to help Buell, and this left him with insufficient force for an advance. But by the end of October all danger from Bragg was past. Grant's strength had been brought up to nearly 50,000, with hopes of further reinforcements, and he felt himself in a position to make a move.

At this time the only stretch of the Mississippi held by the Confederates was from Vicksburg to Port Hudson (200 miles). New Orleans, at the mouth of the river, had been occupied on May 1st as the result of fine work by the U.S. fleet under Admiral Farragut. Some ships had actually run up to Vicksburg, first in May and again in June, taking a few troops with them ; but it was clear that the naval guns could do little harm to the batteries of the town and the attempts were abandoned. The Confederates, seeing the danger, completed the defences of Vicksburg and built other forts down the river, the southernmost being Port Hudson.

The natural strength of Vicksburg was immense. The town stood on a bluff which rose up a couple of hundred feet above the bank ; this made it secure from any assault from the west. Approach from the north was equally impossible on account of the network of bayous or creeks which cover the marshes. The problem was therefore to get a footing on the hard ground on the east or south. The river was the easiest means of approach, but a glance at the map shows that it makes a bend which brings it under fire from the town for a stretch of five or six miles.

December 1862. Grant's first plan was to make a combined movement by land and water, as at Fort

Henry. Sherman with 32,000 men was to go down the
river, escorted by the gunboats, and make a surprise
attack on the height at the north end of the town,
while Grant distracted the attention of the enemy by
a move down the railroad from Memphis. This
attempt was a complete failure. Sherman's surprise
did not succeed, and he was repulsed with a loss of
nearly 2,000. The Confederate cavalry swung round
behind Grant, cut the railways and destroyed his depot
of supplies at Holly Springs. He was obliged to fall
back.

January–March 1863. After this failure several
schemes were devised to cut canals and join up the
creeks with a view to getting the forces within striking
distance of the town.   In spite of every artifice which
the engineers could suggest, and the expenditure of
much labour, all these efforts came to nothing. The
army was brought over to the west bank, opposite
Vicksburg—where there was much difficulty in finding
camps in the swamps—but it seemed impossible to get
any farther.

Grant himself says, ' The strategical way according
to the rule would have been to go back to Memphis,
establish that as a base of supplies and move from there
along the line of the railroad.' This, however, would
be a confession of failure and must intensify the gloom
which had spread over the North. He felt he must go
forward.

The plan of advance was entirely his own ; he consulted nobody, and trusted for approval from Washington after he had set it in motion. The troops on the
west bank worked their way through many hardships
to a point on the river some 30 miles below Vicksburg,
arriving there at the end of April. They were still on
the west bank and required the assistance of the fleet
to take them across. On the night of April 16th the

fleet, under Admiral Porter, made a dash past the batteries of the town. Seven warships and two transports got through—only one transport was lost. On the night of the 22nd other transports got through with ammunition and supplies.

After much reconnaissance to find a suitable crossing-place it was decided to ferry the army over to the east bank at Bruinsburg, and this was done without loss by May 1st.

This gave the Unionists a good place for jumping off, but the fighting was yet to be done. The Confederates could have no doubts about the direction from which the attack would come. The garrison of Vicksburg was believed to amount to about 40,000 under Pemberton, while J. E. Johnston was collecting another force at Jackson, thirty-five miles to the east.

By bringing up every available man Grant's army now mustered 43,000. Taking five days' rations in haversacks and supplementing them with local supplies, he cut himself off from his base and started inland. The first object was to cut in between Vicksburg and Jackson and defeat his enemies in detail.

May 12th. A Confederate force was met at Raymond and driven back on Jackson.

May 14th. Jackson, the capital of the State of Mississippi, was taken. The force under J. E. Johnston, after some resistance, fled northwards, leaving thirty-five guns, some prisoners, and supplies in the hands of the Federals. Grant now turned round to march on Vicksburg.

May 16th. Pemberton had come some way out of the town and occupied a position at Champion's Hill. After serious fighting he was driven back. One of his divisions got away to the south, but the rest fell back towards the town.

May 17th. The Confederates made another weak attempt at resistance, on the Black River, after which they again fell back, and by the evening they were practically shut up in Vicksburg.

May 19th. Grant made an effort to carry the place by assault, and repeated it on the 22nd, but the Confederates fought well behind their parapets and repulsed the storming parties with heavy loss. Nothing remained but to reduce it by regular siege. The Federals had now regained touch with their fleet, on the north side of the town, and so had no difficulties about the transport of supplies and reinforcements. In a short time Grant's force was brought up to 70,000 and there was no anxiety about any attempt which Johnston might make from the outside to relieve the defenders.

July 4th, 1863. The tale of the siege has been told many times : forty-five days of bombardment, sickness, starvation. On July 4th Pemberton surrendered with 30,000 men who were released on parole. As a result of this Port Hudson was also surrendered five days later to a force under Banks. This cleared the whole course of the Mississippi—' The Father of Waters again goes unvexed to the sea.'

Infinite credit was due to the whole of the Union troops who had spent eight very bad months on the way to their victory. But at the same time it was distinctly a personal triumph for Grant ; without him it would never have been carried through, in fact without him the successful phase of the operations would never have been begun. As he himself said, it was not according to rule—it was a triumph of the boldness and perseverance which can afford to break rules.

And if it was a personal triumph for Grant then Lincoln must be given a share of it. Lincoln had boldness and perseverance to stick to a man against

evil report. There is the charm of absolute simplicity
in his summing up of Grant : ' We can't spare this
man ; he fights.'

One more point deserves notice. When Grant got
a footing to the south of Vicksburg, Banks was moving
on Port Hudson. Lincoln thought that the best plan
would be for Grant to go down and join Banks ;
together they would take Port Hudson, and this would
open the Mississippi to Farragut's fleet ; after that the
combined forces could return to attack Vicksburg.
The idea was sound enough—but would of course take
time. Grant saw that the enemy would use this time
to improve fortifications and collect men, and so,
when he came back with a larger force, he would find
a more difficult task in front of him. This determined
him to strike at once, and without waiting for approval
from Washington he set out on the march which, as
we have seen, was completely successful. Lincoln
immediately wrote to admit that Grant had been right
and he himself had been wrong. These were not mere
words of graceful congratulation, they were the
expression of an opinion which Lincoln formed at the
time and to which he clung to the end of the war.
In forming this opinion he was not carried away by the
exciting news of victory. The difference between the
cases of Gettysburg and Vicksburg remained clear :
Meade had fought well, but the battle had been forced
upon him, and after it he had missed an opportunity
which to Lincoln seemed obvious : Grant had made
an opportunity for himself which was obvious to no
one but himself.

The Advance on Chattanooga. Though he did not
interfere with Grant's plans, Lincoln was not content
to be a passive spectator, so he tried his best to assist
by keeping up the pressure at other points. In this,
however, he was not successful owing to the slowness

of his generals. Burnside had been given a command in Ohio and was now ordered to make the advance on Knoxville which had been urged on Buell in January 1862. After much delay he set out from Cincinnati and reached Knoxville on September 1st.

Much more important was the move of Rosecrans on Chattanooga. This was intended to put pressure on Bragg, whose army was the most formidable of the Confederate forces in the West ; at the same time it aimed at the occupation of the key to Eastern Tennessee and the gateway to the South.

The Confederates were fully alive to the value of Chattanooga. Bragg entrenched positions to hold all the approaches from the north and west, and sent his cavalry on raids to cut railways and upset the enemy's preparations.

We left Rosecrans at Nashville in January 1863 after the battle of Murfreesboro. His action varied from very bad to very good and back again with sudden changes which leave us puzzled. There can be little doubt that for the first six months of 1863 his action was bad, or, to put it more correctly, he took no action at all. In spite of constant and urgent appeals from Washington he would not budge. Perhaps he believed the expedition against Vicksburg to be doomed to destruction : if Grant's army met with a decisive reverse it would place the Federals in the West in a precarious situation and throw them on the defensive : in such circumstances it would be better to have Rosecrans' own army well in hand in a central position at Nashville instead of committing it to an offensive movement which might have to be recalled in haste. But if such was the idea at the back of his mind he had not the courage to put it frankly before the authorities at Washington. He excused his inaction by the usual complaints about lack of men, of horses, of supplies— which must have reminded Lincoln of McClellan.

June–September 1863. When Grant completed the investment of Vicksburg it became clear that, so far from being in any danger, he was on the road to an important success. Seeing this, on June 23rd Rosecrans at last began to move—and was at his best. He could put 65,000 into the field against some 40,000. He had studied the ground and, having no intention of attacking the strong positions held by Bragg, set himself to manœuvre. With fine daring he spread out his forces in a manner worthy of Lee. Several feints were made—not half-hearted reconnaissances, but sharp resolute moves which entirely deceived Bragg and ' kept him guessing '. Information was collected quickly, and quick action was taken on it. In the course of nine days the Confederates were forced to abandon their first strong line, then a second, and then to retire over the broad stream of the Tennessee into the town of Chattanooga.

Again Rosecrans had a bad spell of inaction for six weeks. Then, by another bold feint, he kept Bragg looking toward the north while the Federal main body crossed the river, west of the town, and occupied the heights on the south of it. This seriously threatened the enemy's rear—and without striking a blow they made off southwards, leaving Rosecrans to march into the town on September the 9th. His manœuvres had forced the Confederates out of three very strong lines at a cost of less than 1,000 men to himself.

Chickamauga. September 19th, 20th. Bragg had left Chattanooga because the recent case of Vicksburg taught him the folly of clinging to a point, however strong it might appear. But he had no idea of running away : reinforcements were joining him : Longstreet's Corps from Virginia : some of Johnston's troops from near Vicksburg. When he saw that the Federals had spread out widely among the mountains, he turned against them hoping to catch an isolated Corps. In this he failed, because Rosecrans suddenly realized the danger and succeeded in concentrating in the valley of the Chickamauga, which runs into the Tennessee from the south. Though disappointed at finding the Federal Corps united, Bragg faced them and on September 19th an accidental encounter between two leading brigades gradually drew both armies into a general engagement. The fighting was fierce but indecisive.

At 10 a.m. next morning the Confederates resumed their attack. This was one of Rosecrans' bad days. In trying to reinforce the left of his line he gave a very injudicious order which left a gap in the centre. The Southerners saw their opportunity and made the most of it ; they dashed into the opening and routed the whole of the Federal right wing, which fled in confusion to Chattanooga. Rosecrans himself was swept away in the stream of fugitives, and the battle seemed to be a disaster.

Thomas, however, kept his Corps steady on the left ; until night came on he held his ground and earned a title, ' The Rock of Chickamauga,' which places him beside ' Stonewall ' in the roll of fame. Again and again the southern masses hurled themselves against his line—but the only result was to earn for this day the unenviable distinction of being the bloodiest in the whole war. The Federals lost 11,000, the Confederates about 17,000, exclusive of prisoners and missing.

The South claimed victory, as they were left in possession of the field, but they were quite unable to press this advantage. Rosecrans took up a position immediately south of the town. He could hold out there—but the enemy was strong enough to send troops to threaten both flanks, depriving them of all lines of supply except one pass leading over the mountains to the north. For the next month he was practically besieged.

BRAXTON BRAGG (1817–1876)
General, C.S.A.

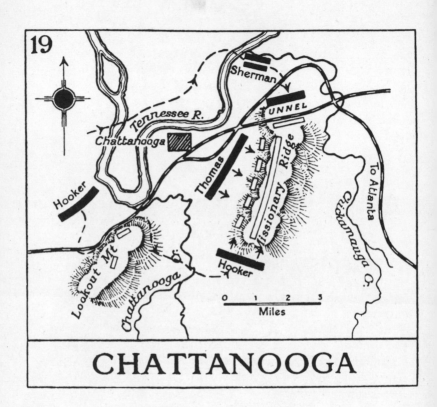

CHATTANOOGA

Grant in command. The news from Chattanooga was sufficiently disturbing to demand strong action in Washington. But this time Lincoln had a simple solution for his difficulties—Grant was summoned to Louisville and Mr. Stanton was sent to meet him, carrying an order which placed him in control of all the forces west of the Alleghanies. At the same time the choice was given him between retaining Rosecrans and replacing him with Thomas; he chose the latter.

An urgent telegram was dispatched ordering Thomas to assume command in Chattanooga and to hold out at all costs; then Grant hastened to the spot himself. He was very lame, through a fall from a horse, but in spite of this he rode the last stages of his journey and arrived in Chattanooga on October 23rd.

He found the Federal troops half starved, so his first object was to regain use of the railways for supplies. Two Corps from Virginia, under Hooker, had been sent as reinforcements; these cleared the roads and railway leading into the town from the west, which enabled full rations to be served out to the hungry garrison.

At this moment Bragg made a bad mistake; he thought he was strong enough to hold his position facing the town and at the same time to detach Longstreet with 20,000 on an expedition to Knoxville. Burnside had been there since September 1st but was running out of ammunition and supplies.

Lincoln sent desperate appeals to Grant to relieve Burnside—and this raised a delicate problem. Grant had men to send, but no transport for them; and as Burnside was already starving, any addition to his force would only add to the starvation. Some means must therefore be taken to ensure the recall of Longstreet, and this could only be done by attacking Bragg. Before doing this it was necessary to wait for the reinforcements which Sherman was bringing up in all haste from the Mississippi.

Grant made his calculations with coolness and courage ; promised Burnside relief ; drew out plans for attacking Bragg—and by November 23rd all was ready.

Battle of Chattanooga, 24th and 25th November 1863.
The arrival of Sherman brought the Federals up to 60,000 against 33,000 Confederates ; but the latter had been given time to establish themselves very strongly. Their main position was on Missionary Ridge, a couple of miles south-east of the town, covering the railroad which runs southward to Atlanta. This ridge, which rose to 800 feet above the valley, was well adapted for defence, its northern flank resting on the Chickamauga Creek. Lookout Mountain, which towers up over 2,000 feet, was held by a detachment of six brigades and seemed to make the left flank secure.

Grant's plan was to send Sherman along the north bank of the Tennessee, but out of sight of the enemy, to a point some four miles above the town ; there he was to be ferried across the river in pontoons ; this would bring him in position to attack the north end of Missionary Ridge. Thomas was to advance straight from the town against the centre of the Ridge. Hooker, coming from farther west, was to climb over Lookout Mountain and form the right.

On November 24th Hooker advanced to fight his famous ' Battle above the Clouds '. The mountain sides were wreathed in heavy mists which prevented the Confederates from having any notion of what was happening. Hooker's men crawled up the ravines and, by pushing their flanks forward, threatened the retreat of those who held the northern extremity of the height. After some resistance the Confederates fell back down the east side and joined their main body on

Missionary Ridge. By the time Hooker had reached the Chattanooga Creek it was dark, so he bivouacked on the west bank.

On the same day Sherman got across the Tennessee. On the 25th Sherman was the first to come into action, and gained ground towards the tunnel. Bragg saw that this move threatened his rear and therefore turned his reserves to repel it. Grant did not wish to launch his attack against the centre until Hooker had come in on the south ; but Hooker was much delayed in getting over the Chattanooga Creek. Thus Sherman's force was the only one in action, and not only failed to advance, but was in danger of being driven back. His situation was so serious that at 3 p.m. Grant had to give the order for Thomas to assault, without waiting for Hooker. This led to the most glorious charge of the war.

In addition to holding the crest of the Ridge, Bragg had placed a row of rifle pits at the foot of it. Grant intended Thomas to take this and then halt to reform. But, having rushed the Confederates out of this first line, the gallant troops of Thomas were in no mood to halt ; close on the heels of the enemy they went on, without orders, in fact against orders, right up the steep face of the Ridge, right into the second line, right over it. The Confederate centre was broken and they fell back, utterly routed, leaving many prisoners and guns behind them.

Considering the strength of Bragg's position the casualties were not so heavy as might have been expected. The Federals lost 5,500 ; the Confederates 3,000 killed and wounded, 6,000 prisoners, and 40 guns.

In his *Memoirs* Grant ascribes the success to Bragg's mistakes, first in sending away Longstreet to Knoxville, and second, on the battle-field, in putting an advanced line at the base of the Ridge ; while the Confederates were retiring from this line they prevented the troops on the crest from firing on the Federals who were close behind them.

Chattanooga was one of the most decisive battles of the war.

As soon as it was evident that Bragg's defeat was complete, Grant turned his attention to the relief of Burnside. This was accomplished without further fighting. Sherman was directed toward Knoxville with two divisions, and Longstreet cleared off to the eastward on his approach.

XIX

1864

Situation, January 1864.

THE victories of Gettysburg, Vicksburg, and Chattanooga had placed the Federal armies on a long
and firm line from the Potomac, through Western
Virginia, to Knoxville and Chattanooga, thence to
Memphis and down the Mississippi. The blockade
was growing tighter. It is the general opinion of
historians that President Davis ought to have abandoned so hopeless a struggle and that heavy responsibility lies on his shoulders for the continuance of bloodshed. Military writers suggest that the South had
still a hope, rather a forlorn hope, in staking everything
on a big offensive movement ; this meant giving up all
attempt to hold on to the ports and territories still in
the hands of Confederate forces, concentrating every
available man under Lee, and trusting him to spread
such terror and devastation in the North that it would
raise a demand for the suspension of hostilities. From
a military point of view the idea is attractive, and it
would certainly have appealed to Stonewall Jackson.
Two years earlier it might have been something more
than a forlorn hope. But the Southern President had
missed his chances when he refused to give Lee sufficient
troops for the former invasions ; he clung obstinately
to the belief that a defensive attitude would wear out
the patience of the Northerners. He was not far wrong
as regards some of them—but he was dead wrong about
those who counted, including Grant, the Union Army,
and Lincoln.

The victories in the last six months of '63 had done
something more than place the Federals on a strong

line ; they had produced well-tried generals. The great soldiers of the Union, except those who had very direct dealings with Lincoln, have not come into this story, but it is certainly not from any failure on my part to recognize their abilities.

To the President the victories brought real personal relief in the shape of a General on whom he could rely and who was accepted without hesitation by the army and the nation. On former occasions he had made up his own mind, but could scarcely avoid the feeling that his choice might arouse jealousy or misgivings. It must have been a comfort to know that, though he himself was being criticized and abused, the man at the head of the army was hailed with enthusiasm by all parties. Congress passed the necessary Act to revive the obsolete rank of Lieutenant-General ; the Senate confirmed the President's nomination—and Grant was summoned to Washington.

On March 9th Lincoln and Grant met for the first time. It was a formal reception for the purpose of handing his commission to the new Lieutenant-General ; the speeches were formal in tone.

Next day they had a private talk, and I think it must have been disappointing to both of them. Grant recounts it :

' In my first interview with Mr. Lincoln alone he stated to me that he had never professed to be a military man or to know how campaigns should be conducted, and never wanted to interfere in them : but that procrastination on the part of commanders and the pressure of the people of the North and Congress, which was always with him, forced him into issuing his series of Military Orders. He did not know but they were all wrong, and did know that some of them were. All he wanted or had ever wanted was someone who would take the responsibility and act, and call on him for all the assistance needed, pledging himself to use all the power of the Government in rendering such assistance. Assuring him that I would do the best I could with the means at hand, and avoid as far as possible annoying him or the War Department, our first interview ended.'

A pair of thorough Anglo-Saxons. Big fates lay in the hands of these two men ; there were a thousand questions which they ought to have thrashed out and which Lincoln must have been longing to discuss ; the prospects of the war, the staying power of the nation, the ability of the generals, the organization at Washington, the state of the troops, recruiting : a thousand questions about the South and its army. Perhaps Lincoln was over-anxious to allay any suspicions about civilian interference, and so overplayed his part ; his tone may have given the impression that he wanted to wash his hands of all responsibility and hear no more about it. Perhaps Grant was shy ; perhaps he did not see the shrewd insight and the wealth of knowledge that waited not to interfere but to help. They trusted each other, certainly, but did not use each other as they might have done. And so ' our first interview ended ' and Grant has nothing to say about it. His memoirs are discreet, which is creditable to the author but tantalizing to the reader, who knows that there must have been a good deal behind the veil of reserve. Farther on we get a little more light, especially on Stanton :

' There is no great difference of opinion now, in the public mind, as to the characteristics of the President. With Mr. Stanton the case is different. They were the very opposite of each other in almost every particular, except that each possessed great ability. Mr. Lincoln gained influence over men by making them feel that it was a pleasure to serve him. He preferred yielding his own wish to gratify others, rather than to insist on having his own way. It distressed him to disappoint others. In matters of public duty, however, he had what he wished, but in the least offensive way. Mr. Stanton never questioned his own authority to command, unless resisted. He cared nothing for the feelings of others. He felt no hesitation in assuming the functions of the executive or in acting without advising him. If his act was not sustained, he would change it—if he saw the matter would be followed up until he did so. It was generally supposed that these two officials formed the complement of each other. The Secretary was required to prevent the President's being imposed upon. The President was required in the more responsible place of seeing that injustice was not done to others. I do not know that this view of these two men is still entertained by the majority of the people. It is not a correct view, however, in my estimation. Mr. Lincoln did not require a guardian to aid him in the fulfilment of a public trust.'

Lincoln, who ' had what he wished ', looked on quietly while Grant went quietly to work. There were no sweeping changes in organization or appointments. Stanton was allowed to go on in his cantankerous way. Halleck was officially styled what he had really been all along, ' Chief of the Staff ', at Washington. Meade remained officially at the head of the Army of the Potomac, but was really the Chief of Staff in the field, issuing orders in accordance with the plans of Grant, who accompanied the army in person.

Grant says : ' I did not communicate my plans to the President, nor did I to the Secretary of War or General Halleck.'

This closes the chapter of Lincoln's active part as Strategist of the North. But, for a reason which will appear later, it is worth while to take a rough glance at the subsequent events before we take stock of his military ability.

Grant's plan was to make a simultaneous advance with four separate armies :

1. Grant himself, with the Army of the Potomac, 120,000 strong, was to bring Lee to action by marching towards Richmond.

2. A force of 15,000 under Sigel was to move southward in the Shenandoah Valley.

3. Butler, with two Corps, 35,000, was to make a show on the Peninsula, to delude Lee into the belief that the main attack would come that way. Then he was to cross over the James River and aim at Richmond from the south.

4. Sherman, who succeeded Grant as commander in

ROBERT EDWARD LEE (1807–1870)
General, C.S.A.

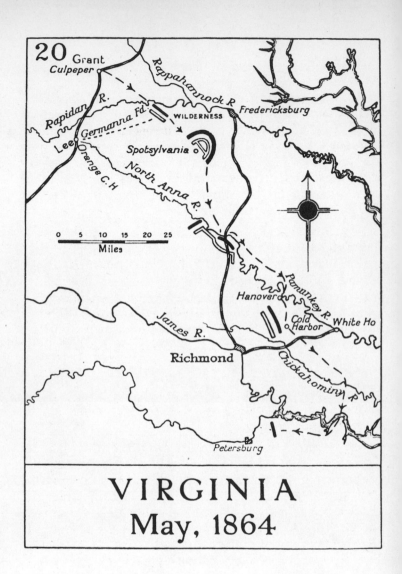

VIRGINIA
May, 1864

the West, was to advance from Chattanooga towards Atlanta.

All four armies were to start operations on May 4th. It may be said at once that Butler's effort was useless owing to the incapacity of Butler himself. He reached the south bank of the James at Bermuda, but never got any farther. The effort in the Valley was also feeble, and nothing effective was done there till Sheridan took up the command in August. The heavy fighting in the East was done by Grant.

The Campaign in Virginia. After Gettysburg Meade had followed Lee steadily, but nothing of importance took place during the winter. In April Lee was holding the line of the Rapidan, facing the Federal main body which lay round Culpeper (see Sketch 20). Nothing would have pleased Grant better than an attempt by Lee to break away to the north, where there might be a chance of catching him in the open ; but there were no signs of such intention.

Grant had 120,000 men in four Corps (Hancock, Warren, Sedgwick, and Burnside), with 9,000 cavalry under Sheridan. Lee's main body was believed to muster about 60,000.

May 3rd. Grant began to cross the Rapidan at Germanna. Lee made no attempt to oppose the passage of the river ; Longstreet, who had been called up from East Tennessee, was not yet in line ; in addition to this the wooded ground on the south bank of the river suited the Confederates, who knew it well, while it prevented the Federals making full use of their powerful artillery. But on hearing of Grant's move, Lee marched eastwards, and the first battle was a few miles south of the river.

May 5th, 6th. The Wilderness. Grant had hoped to get through the woods into more open ground ; but finding that Lee was close to him he turned to attack.

Lee also intended to attack. The result was a succession
of assaults and counter-assaults with little progress on
either side. On the second day Hancock was gaining
ground on the left when Longstreet arrived and drove
him back to his original line. It is curious that Longstreet himself was wounded by a shot from one of his
own men not far from the spot where Jackson had fallen
in the same way just a year before.

Late on the 6th Lee attacked the Federal right. There
were no decisive results.

Grant now decided to move eastward, hoping to get
round Lee's right flank. At the same time he sent
Sheridan with most of the cavalry, which was of little
use in the Wilderness, to raid the enemy's rear. Passing
round by the east he tore up some ten miles of railroad
between Lee and Richmond, and captured a large
amount of stores. He had some sharp skirmishes with
the Confederate cavalry, in one of which Stuart was
killed.

May 8th–19th. Spotsylvania. Lee had anticipated
Grant's move to the east, and when the leading Federal
troops approached Spotsylvania Court House they
found it already occupied by the enemy. The drawn-
out battle which followed was at very close quarters—
an affair of breastworks and bayonet charges, with guns
here and there firing point blank with canister.

Grant continued to take troops from his right and
send them round behind the centre to prolong the left.
Gradually they worked round till Lee had to bend back
his right flank in a sharp angle to meet them. The position was not unlike the Ypres Salient in 1914, and the
fighting was something of the same fierce and ragged
kind : higher commanders knowing little of what was
going on : subalterns with handfuls of men doing the
big work which nobody has ever heard of.

On the 10th Colonel Upton made a famous assault on

the ' Bloody Angle ', and got in, but had to fall back from lack of supports.

On the 11th Grant wrote to Washington : ' We have now ended the sixth day of very hard fighting—I purpose to fight it out on this line if it takes all summer.' It took longer than that.

On the 13th Lee abandoned the point of the Bloody Angle and took up a fresh line across its base.

By the 19th the continuous movement of Grant by the east forced Lee to withdraw behind the North Anna River.

The Federals got across this river both east and west of their enemy, but found his entrenchments so formidable that Grant made yet another effort to manœuvre him out of them, so as to get to grips in the open. But while Grant was moving round on an outside circle, Lee, on the inside, could always keep between him and Richmond.

On the 28th the Federals crossed the Pamunkey at Hanover Town, but found the enemy still facing them. The two sides were in close touch, and skirmishing was incessant.

June 3rd. Cold Harbor. With the assistance of the navy, Grant had shifted his base to White House. He ordered Butler, who was south of the James River, to send up Smith's Corps by water to join the main body ; it arrived on May 31st. By June 2nd Grant had worked his way to Cold Harbor. As he had failed to get round Lee, who was found to be facing him with a line of entrenchments, his patience was exhausted and he delivered a frontal attack. The Federals had no chance against the strong line, and were flung back with appalling slaughter. Grant admits that he regretted this battle : ' No advantage whatever was gained to compensate for the heavy loss we sustained.'

From the 3rd to the 12th of June the two armies lay

opposite each other. Then Grant made a very skilful march, and crossed the Chickahominy and James Rivers. On the 15th the leading troops joined Butler, who for some time had been facing the fortifications on the east side of Petersburg. From the 15th to the 18th heavy assaults were made, as it was hoped that Lee had not yet discovered the move to the south bank of the James. As a matter of fact Lee did not discover it till the 17th, but the lines of Petersburg were strong enough to resist assault, even with a thin garrison, and the Federal storming parties were thrown back with a loss of 10,000 men.

This convinced Grant of the futility of further attacks, and, as at Vicksburg, he sat down to regular siege operations which lasted well into the next year. An attempt was made to open a breach with the help of a mine ; this was exploded on July 30th, with much effect, but the arrangements to follow up the success were thoroughly bad, and in the end the Federals fell back, with a loss of 4,000 men. The fiasco was so complete that a Court of Inquiry was held to examine into the causes of it.

In the grim duel between Grant and Lee the losses were terrible. Some 60,000 Federals, the best in the army, had fallen. On the Confederate side the numbers are not known, but they were certainly not so high. There was a strong feeling in the North that Grant had failed.

The attack at Cold Harbor was a distinct mistake— but some light is thrown back on the other operations by events of the Great War. After the battle of the Aisne the Germans persistently extended their right towards the north, hoping to double round the left flank of the Allies : to meet them the Allies gradually extended their line till it reached as far north as Ypres. Everywhere the Germans found themselves forced to make frontal attacks which, at most, gained a few yards of ground. Supports were hurried up on both sides, entrenchments were dug, barbed wire was put up, and the long deadlock began. After that frontal attacks, often on a small and sometimes on a large scale, kept up the pressure—it was a war of attrition.

In the same way we see Grant trying to work round a flank—but Lee always managed to face him. The Confederates had learnt the stopping power of entrenchments and obstacles, and the attacks were therefore costly. Grant, however, could afford to force the fighting and his blunt attacks gained two advantages. First, the Confederates were worn down far more than appears from a roll of casualties ; when not fighting they were marching, and when not marching they were digging ; the next heavy blow might come at any moment. Second, Lee did not dare to make wide movements as at Second Bull Run and Chancellorsville: it has been said that this was because he no longer had a Jackson to carry them out, but to this may be added that he no longer had a Hooker against him : he knew that if he divided his forces Grant would crush whatever was left nearest to him ; he had to keep his men together and conform to the movements of his adversary instead of initiating manœuvres of his own.

The heavy fighting had therefore considerable effect —but as soon as it was relaxed, that is, after Cold Harbor, Lee could revert to his old methods ; he felt himself safe enough in his lines for the time being, and could afford to make a diversion. It is difficult to say why Grant did not foresee this. The garrison of Washington had been depleted to fill up the gaps in the front line, till it was reduced to 20,000 raw recruits and invalids. When Grant went to the south bank of the James there was practically nothing between Richmond and Washington : he was right in believing that Lee would not abandon the Southern Capital and go north in force—but he might have known that Lee would not sit entirely quiet.

.   .   .   .

Early's Raid. When the main advance was launched into the Wilderness, Sigel got orders to move southwards in the Shenandoah Valley. After some unimportant engagements he was forced back to Strasburg, and there he was relieved by Hunter. On May 28th Hunter started southwards with 9,000 men and defeated a Confederate force near Staunton on June 5th. Here he was joined by another 10,000 who had been working up from the south-west under Crook and Averell. He then pushed forward towards Lynchburg (fifty miles south of Staunton).

At this moment, however, Lee's diversion began to take effect. Early's Corps had left Richmond on June 13th, arrived at Lynchburg in time to defend that town, and drove Hunter back. The latter, fearing that his retreat by the Valley might be cut off, retired away into the mountains of West Virginia, and disappeared.

The enterprising Early now made up his mind to invade the North. He had 17,000 men. Without opposition he made his way to the Potomac, crossed it at Shepherdstown, and reached Frederick City on July 9th. Continuing his march he drove off a weak detachment which was sent to meet him under Lew Wallace. On July 11th he appeared before the forts on the north-west side of Washington.

It is generally admitted by Northern writers that if Early had moved a little quicker after crossing the Potomac and had known the weak state of the garrison he could have got into the city; though he was not strong enough to hold it there was plenty of mischief to be done even in twenty-four hours.

Grant, at Petersburg, was very slow in the uptake. It was not until Early had crossed the Potomac that he began to realize the danger and send troops to reinforce the garrison ; even then he dribbled them in, one division at a time. Fortunately the leading troops of the 6th Corps arrived at the same time as Early and were able to check him till others came up. After that Washington was safe, and the Confederates had to get back south of the Potomac.

In May '62, Lee had seen that Jackson might be punished for his boldness not only by being driven back, but by being cut off and captured. In the same way he now saw that Early would not be allowed to escape unharmed. By July 13th the Federals had ample strength within call : the 6th and 19th Corps were in Washington : Hunter's force had made its roundabout way to Martinsburg, at the north end of the Valley. True to his self-imposed restraint, the President did not take command, but suggested that Grant should come and do so—' this is what I think, and is not an order '.

The situation in Washington during this month shows the necessity of having one responsible Commander-in-Chief in a position well outside the firing line. Lincoln did not want to give orders which might clash with Grant's. Grant was too far away to make quick decisions. Halleck would issue only such orders as he got from Grant. No one else had any authority to concert the scattered forces of the Union.

The result was a lot of telegraphing in a game of cross purposes—which left Early at liberty not only to escape but to pursue further adventures. He went first to Strasburg, then turned north again, drove back a weak body of Federals under Crook, and sent his cavalry under McCausland to raid Maryland. McCausland got as far as Chambersburg on July 30th, and as that town could not ransom itself, he set it on fire ; returning by a devious route he was caught at Moorefield on August 7th and badly defeated by Averell.

On August 1st Grant sent Sheridan to Washington, with the intention of putting him in command of all the troops in that area. And when this was communicated to Lincoln it drew from him an urgent reply :

'*August 3rd.* I have seen your despatch in which you say, " I want Sheridan put in command of all the troops in the field, with instructions to put himself south of the enemy, and follow him to the death." This, I think, is exactly right as to how our forces should move. But please look over the despatches you may have received from here, even since you made that order, and discover, if you can, that there is any idea in the head of anyone here, of putting our army *south* of the enemy, or of following him to the death in any direction. I repeat to you it will neither be done nor attempted unless you watch it every day, and hour, and force it.'

This letter seems to have brought Grant to a sense of his real responsibilities. He went north himself, put Sheridan in Hunter's place, and gave him authority over the 30,000 troops in the area. He then returned to Petersburg—without seeing the President.

I feel sure that if Lincoln and Grant had opened their hearts to each other in the first interview, much of this disorganization might have been avoided. Lincoln could have explained the difficulties which had arisen in the days of McClellan. Grant would have grasped that not only the President but the public insisted on the security of Washington ; he would have left somebody, a Sheridan, to take command in Washington and prevent chaos.

If Early had arrived one day sooner he could have done material damage to the Treasury and banks, to the arsenals and stores, and the moral effect would have brought down both the President and Grant in the ruins. The people were prepared to undergo necessary sacrifices, but would find it hard to forgive the quite unnecessary sacrifice of their Capital. There were 200,000 troops in the eastern theatre, compared with whom Early's 17,000 were a small band of raiders.

WILLIAM TECUMSEH SHERMAN (1820–1891)
Lieutenant General, U.S.A.

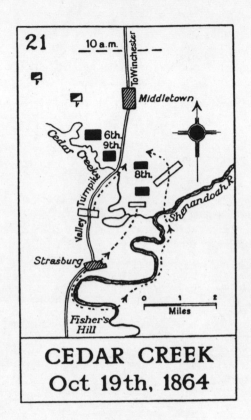

CEDAR CREEK
Oct 19th, 1864

He was easily driven off as soon as the matter was taken in hand. But if he had got in without a blow, the public would have judged very rightly that the military organization was thoroughly incapable.

Sheridan in the Valley. P. H. Sheridan was only thirty-three years of age, but even before the Civil War he had picked up experience against the Indians in the West. Throughout '62 and '63 he had shown his fighting weight, especially at Murfreesboro and Chattanooga. Then, at the head of the cavalry in Virginia, he had given evidence of daring, resourcefulness, and self-confidence. He was an ideal man for a job in the Valley, and Grant atoned for his former carelessness by the wisdom of his choice.

Sheridan, though fearless, was not foolhardy. During August there were reports, well founded, that reinforcements were reaching Early. Grant's pressure on Richmond would force Lee to call them back before long. Therefore with cool calculation Sheridan waited at the north end of the Valley. By September 14th his expectations were fulfilled—Lee had ordered Early to send back one division to Richmond. Sheridan immediately prepared to strike, and Grant, who had again come up to visit him, approved of his plans.

September 19th. Winchester. Sheridan advanced from Snicker's Gap in the Blue Ridge towards Winchester. A few miles outside the town he met Early's force, and after a long day's fighting utterly defeated it and sent it flying southwards.

September 22nd. Fisher's Hill. The Confederates pulled themselves together in a strong position across the Valley, a couple of miles south of Strasburg. Sheridan deceived Early by a feint against his centre, then flung a corps against the left. The Confederates broke and fled in confusion, leaving many prisoners behind them.

Sheridan had no intention of occupying the Valley,

and was anxious to send some of his troops to help
Grant. Therefore, after letting his cavalry go well
south, nearly to Staunton, he turned back. On his
way northward he destroyed barns and mills and left
the fertile valley in a state of devastation.

The Valley had always been the main granary of the
Southern army, and its importance was all the greater
at this moment when many other sources of supply
were cut off. In hopes of keeping it, Lee determined
once more to reinforce Early with a division from
Richmond. Hearing that Sheridan was retiring, Early
only waited for the reinforcements, and then hurried
after him ; the cavalry which formed the vanguard
was completely routed by the Federal cavalry at Wood-
stock, but in spite of this check Early pushed forward
and entered Strasburg on October 14th.

October 19th. Cedar Creek. Sheridan himself had
been called to Washington to discuss the future dis-
position of his troops. He left his army encamped on
the north bank of Cedar Creek.

Early had found the Valley so ravaged that, far from
being a source of supplies for Richmond, it could not
even support the troops on the spot. He must either
attack or retire. With much spirit he chose to attack,
and laid his plans with real skill. More than half of the
Southern forces were sent to make a turning movement
by the east ; twice they had to ford the Shenandoah ;
but, aided by a dense fog, they got into the Federal
left flank and threw it into confusion which spread to
the centre. Victory seemed to be in the hands of the
Confederates.

On the right, however, the 6th Corps stood fast, and
gave time for the defeated troops from the left and
centre to form a line a mile north of Middletown.
Early had to halt and reform before making another
attack.

On his way back from Washington Sheridan had spent the night of the 18th in Winchester. Soon after eight o'clock in the morning he heard reports of heavy gunfire ; he at once got to saddle and started on his famous ride. He was met by a stream of fugitives who had been thrown into panic by Early's surprise attack, but they rallied at his word, and the stream turned back towards the enemy. By 10.30 Sheridan reached the field and took command. A strong line of battle was formed to meet Early's next onset, which was easily repulsed. Then it was Sheridan's turn to take the offensive. There was hard fighting before the Confederates gave way, but once their line was broken the rout was complete. Cedar Creek was one of the most decisive engagements of the war.

Sheridan's active campaign in the Valley had lasted just one month, from September 19th to October 19th. It was a brilliant affair and shut for ever the dangerous ' backdoor to the North '. The later operations in the Valley were of no interest.

Atlanta Campaign. May 4th–September 2nd. While Grant was fighting his way towards Richmond another fierce contest was going on in the west, under the able lieutenant, Sherman, whom he had left to take his place.

W. T. Sherman was forty-four years old. He had passed through West Point and had served as a sub-altern of artillery. After commanding a brigade at First Bull Run, he was transferred to the West, where he became Grant's closest friend and most trusted lieutenant. He was given to express his feelings with freedom, especially about politicians, and fell under the ban of some journalists who went so far as to call him insane. He was a student of the science of war, a man of many sides, eager and restless. Though of a nature very different from Grant's, they exchanged letters which show true friendship and outspoken frankness, which must have been of value to both of them. There was a long consultation between them before Grant left the West, and then Sherman found himself, with a free hand, in command of all the forces at Chattanooga. These amounted to 100,000 men, divided into three armies, under Thomas, McPherson, and Schofield.

From Chattanooga to Atlanta is 120 miles : a single line of rail connects the two towns. The Confederates, 60,000 strong, were commanded by J. E. Johnston, who had succeeded Bragg ; he took up a strong position astride the railroad, thirty miles south of Chattanooga.

The assaults at Vicksburg had taught Sherman the cost of attempts on prepared lines : though anxious to fight he would not fight at a disadvantage, and so his opening move was intended to get Johnston out of his entrenchments. The ground, though hilly and broken, was better suited for wide movements and concerted action than the tangled forest of Virginia. Cavalry could swing out wide ; guns could support infantry ; a commander could see what was going on and had a chance to retain control.

Sherman started on May 4th, at the same time as Grant was entering the Wilderness. The main body pushed up to the enemy's front while McPherson made a sweep round to the west and threatened the railway twenty miles in rear of Johnston. Though the Confederates were not altogether taken by surprise they had to evacuate their first position and fall back to a second one. This manœuvre was repeated again and again. Sherman's turning force was always bold, never too bold ; it always succeeded in threatening the enemy's rear but never quite got on to it. Johnston was cautious, never timid ; when he stood to offer battle Sherman refused to attack, when Sherman advanced to attack Johnston slipped back into a fresh line. It was a duel of keen blades and perfect fencing as compared with the slogging match which was going on in Virginia. Mile by mile Johnston was pressed back, always skirmishing; tearing up the railway and destroying the bridges ; sheltering his men behind stout breastworks and obstacles. Only once Sherman attacked his front, at Keneshaw Mountain, twenty miles north of Atlanta—and was repulsed with loss.

After two and a half months of such work Sherman was in sight of Atlanta, a city of big industries and an important railway junction. He was disappointed in not getting the chance he wanted to fight in the open, but nevertheless the city was in itself a valuable prize if he could take it. While he was preparing plans to get round it, this time by the east, President Davis stepped in to assist him by ordering Johnston to hand over his command to Hood. The Southern President had never been on good terms with Johnston, and, seeing the continuous retreat, took it as a sign of want of enterprise. Sherman, who knew better, was delighted with the change.

Hood was a hard fighter and his impetuosity was well known. He soon gave proof of it. While the Federal forces were spreading round the city he left his entrenchments to attack them, but a local success here and there was dearly paid for. The casualties had always been heaviest on the side of the attackers and this was certainly the case in Hood's attacks.

After cutting the railroad which leads to the east Sherman came round to the other lines which run south-west. This provoked Hood to another attack, which was so costly that President Davis sent orders to stop further attempts of this kind.

Sherman left one Corps to guard the railway on the north side of the city and concentrated all the rest of his force to the south-west, and then to the south. By the end of August he held all the railways and the fate of Atlanta was sealed. On the night of September 1st loud explosions showed that Hood was blowing up magazines and stores—a proof that he meant to evacuate. The Confederate forces slipped away to the south-east, and Sherman took possession of the city on September 2nd.

The casualties during the four months, May to August, came to rather over 30,000 on each side, but those of the South were relatively heavier, besides the loss of Atlanta and the railways.

The March through Georgia. The problem of further operations was not an easy one. Sherman already had behind him 120 miles of vulnerable communications, and had no wish to prolong them by hunting Hood. At the same time he must do something. The solution showed ingenuity : Thomas, with half the army, was sent back to Chattanooga to take a defensive attitude there ; this reduced the line of supply, thereby economizing forces : Sherman himself proposed to march eastward, abandoning communications altogether. This would leave Hood the choice between following Thomas and hitting up against his entrenchments or following Sherman through a country which the latter had completely devastated. Grant did not accept the proposed plan with enthusiasm ; Hood had collected some reinforcements and moved north-west, where he looked threatening. But on November 2nd Sherman got the approval for which he had been waiting—to march ' into the air ', through Georgia, leaving Hood to his own devices and to the care of Thomas.

On November 15th the march began, soldiers singing lustily and plundering energetically. The country was rich enough to feed an army of 60,000 which went straight through, especially when the army had orders to leave nothing eatable behind it. No lines of communication needed. Three hundred miles to the sea. Three hundred miles of desolation left behind. On December 21st Sherman entered Savannah.

Nashville. Dec. 15th–16th. While Sherman went eastwards the impetuous Hood went north ; his intention was to spread such dismay in Tennessee that the Federal authorities would recall Sherman ; leaving Chattanooga on his right he moved towards Nashville.

Thomas collected his forces at Nashville ; this was much farther back than Sherman had intended, and the deliberation of his movements caused growing uneasiness. The authorities at Washington were wondering whether Sherman's departure had been wise, whether Thomas would be able to deal with Hood. The uneasiness of Grant reached such a pitch that after sending urgent telegrams he followed them by sending another general, Logan, to supersede Thomas, and was on the point of starting for Nashville himself when he got better news.

The imperturbable Thomas left one Corps under Schofield to delay the enemy ; this was done with much effect, and heavy casualties were inflicted on Hood as he pressed forward, especially in the battle of Franklin, twenty miles south of Nashville. But the Confederates were not deterred, and they appeared in front of the town on December 2nd. The weather was bad, and Thomas did not hurry himself. But on December 15th he moved out and hit hard, forcing Hood back a couple of miles ; next day he hit harder and gained a really decisive victory. 4,500 prisoners and 53 guns fell into his hands. The actual casualties were fairly equal, amounting to some 3,000 on each side.

The Election. The thunder of the guns in those momentous months of 1864 was not loud enough to drown the clamour of politics. A presidential election was due in November, and it was fairly evident that if the Democrats won there would be some attempt at a compromise with the South.

In June the Republican Convention nominated Lincoln as candidate, but the course of the war in July, the losses at Petersburg, and Early's raid plunged the country into deep gloom. There were clever men who honestly believed that the only hope of the Republican party lay in finding a stronger candidate than Lincoln ; it was openly hinted that he ought to withdraw ; the names of Chase, Butler, Grant, and Fremont were mentioned ; a revolt in the party was within the bounds of possibility.

The Democrats held their convention in August at Chicago. For some time it had been known that McClellan would be selected as their candidate. Apparently they had a united front, but there were deep differences below the surface. Governor Seymour, of New York, presided over the convention ; a man of high patriotism, in favour of continuing the war. Vallandigham, after imprisonment and other escapades, had been allowed to return, and was the leader of those who demanded immediate peace. But the desire to defeat Lincoln brought them on to a common platform. Vallandigham and the peace party were allowed to pass a resolution which the public soon reduced to a terse phrase, ' Resolved that the war is a failure.' Seymour and the war party were allowed to nominate their candidate, McClellan, whose letter of acceptance disavowed the resolution. This delightful compromise was intended to ease the conscience of those who were bothered with principles—a peace fanatic could cling to the Resolution while a war fanatic kept his eye on McClellan ; all that mattered was that both should vote Democratic.

But scarcely had they resolved that war was a failure when news arrived of the capture of Atlanta. There

was something definite about this which everybody
could get hold of. It was followed by the victories of
Sheridan in the Valley. The Democrats had committed themselves to the ' failure ', the Republicans
caught up the phrase and put it side by side with the
dispatches of Sherman and Sheridan. Nothing more
was said about Lincoln's resignation.

The men who had fought for three years were in no
mood to surrender when victory was within sight, and
they said so in unmistakable terms. On November 8th
Lincoln was elected President for the second time ;
he got 212 votes, McClellan got 21. It was one of
those decisions which sustain our faith in the sanity
of Anglo-Saxons.

XX

THE LAST PHASE

Situation in January, 1865.

LEE'S army in Richmond was now the only remaining force of the South which counted for anything. Hood's army in the West had been dispersed by defeat at Nashville ; Johnston was sent to rally the remnants and in March he had collected about 30,000 men in North Carolina, but they were badly organized and poorly equipped.

In August 1864 the blockade had been advanced a stage by the capture of the forts at Mobile ; this was the wonderful naval exploit of gallant old Admiral Farragut. By the end of the year Charleston and Wilmington were the only ports of value in the hands of the Confederates : both were taken by the Federals in February 1865.

There were small garrisons at a few places inland such as Lynchburg : some guerrilla bands, under leaders like Forrest and Mosbey, were still at large, but they had no effect on the major operations.

At Richmond the Federals were firmly established close up to the fortifications on the east and south sides, but they had not sufficient force to extend their siege lines to the west. Thus two lines of railway were still open, to bring into the city the scanty supplies which could still be collected outside.

Lee's situation was desperate. We know now that he wanted to break out to the south-west and join Johnston, but his horses were starved and the state of the roads made movement impossible till the worst months of winter were over.

Sherman in the Carolinas. The march through Georgia was of questionable value. It certainly brought home to the inhabitants the stern realities of war, and destroyed a large quantity of the dwindling resources of the South. But it did not draw off any Confederate troops, and when Sherman reached Savannah on December 21st there was no enemy within three hundred miles of him. According to all the rules of strategy he should have been transferred, as quickly as possible, to some point where his 60,000 veterans could pull their weight. This might have been done : the U.S. Navy had plenty of experience in transporting troops by sea, and could have landed them near Richmond in the early days of January. With their assistance Grant could have completed the investment of the city.

Instead of this Sherman went by land, through the Carolinas. As a march it was a fine performance—450 miles in fifty days, bad weather, bad roads, broken bridges. He occupied important towns, Columbia, Goldsboro', and he did further damage to the resources of the South. But for a couple of months his army was wasted as a fighting force. It is true that in March he attracted the attention of Johnston ; but the latter had never any intention of going into Richmond, where he would only have increased the starvation. It is also true that the Army of the Potomac was equal to the task of defeating Lee without Sherman's aid. But Grant's own words show that he went through anxious days in February and March, when Sherman's help would surely have been acceptable.

' One of the most anxious periods of my experience during the rebellion was the last few weeks before Petersburg. I felt that the situation of the Confederates was such that they would try to make an escape at the earliest practicable moment, and I was afraid, every morning, that I would awake from my sleep to hear that Lee had gone.'

Just before the end Lincoln came to visit Grant at
City Point on the James River, and Grant says :

' Mr. Lincoln knew that it had been arranged for Sherman to
join me at a fixed time, to co-operate in the destruction of Lee's
army. I told him that I had been very anxious to have the
Eastern armies vanquish their old enemy who had so long
resisted all their repeated and gallant attempts to subdue them
or drive them from their Capital. The Western armies had been
in the main successful, and were now almost ready to knock at
the back door of Richmond, asking admittance. I said to him
that if the Western armies should be even on the field, operating
against Richmond and Lee, the credit would be given to them
for the capture, by politicians and non-combatants from the
section of the country which those troops hailed from. It
might lead to disagreeable bickerings between members of
Congress from the East and those of the West. Mr. Lincoln
said he saw that now, but had never thought of it before, because his anxiety was so great that he did not care where the
aid came from so the work was done.'

The idea of leaving the Army of the Potomac to
finish off its own job is all very well for stage heroes,[1]
but is too thin to be a factor in practical strategy. It
is impossible to get away from the feeling that there was
something else behind, of which we know nothing.
Sherman's memoirs afford no clue.

Sheridan's march of devastation through the Valley
was quite another thing. It made the road to the
North impassable for a force of any size. This was a
practical step for the defence of the North. But as
soon as his work was done he was ordered to join
Grant. For some time the roads were too bad for his
cavalry, and it was not till near the end of February
that he could start. He marched to Staunton, and was
intending to go on to Lynchburg so as to approach
Richmond from the west. But incessant rains hampered his movements and left the rivers in flood ;
therefore he turned eastward from Staunton, passed

---

[1] See Shakespeare's *Henry V*, Act IV, Sc. iii.

JOSEPH EGGLESTON JOHNSTON (1807–1891)
General, C.S.A.

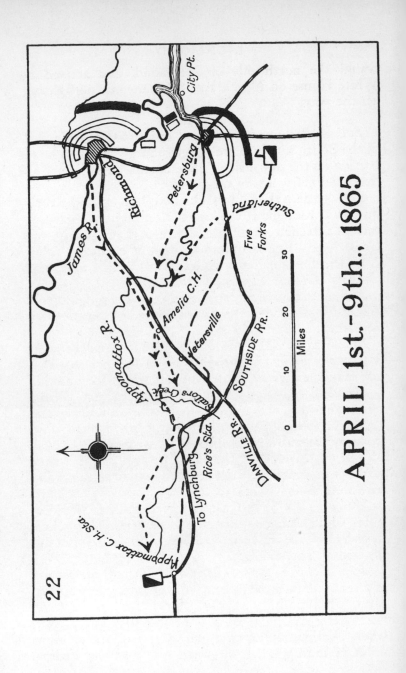

APRIL 1st.-9th., 1865

22

round the north side of Richmond, and arrived at White House on March 19th. There was no fighting on the way.

Fall of Richmond. Lee had converted the Capital of the South into a fortress, Petersburg forming a large bastion on the south side. (See Sketch 22.) The lines extended thirty-seven miles.

Facing them the Federals had built an equally strong line, and throughout the long winter months there was waged a trench warfare not unlike that seen in the Great War. Practically no changes of position.

In the final operations Grant was at his best, and Grant's best was very good indeed.

March 26th. Sheridan's cavalry was brought from White House across the James River to the south of Petersburg.

March 27th. Three infantry divisions were brought from the north to the south bank of the James. This left only one division facing the east side of Richmond.

March 29th. Sheridan, with all his cavalry, swung out to the west, threatening the Southside Railway and the extreme right of the enemy's entrenchments. Two infantry Corps were to follow. There was a skirmish on the 30th near Five Forks. Lee saw that his flank was in danger and sent infantry to support the cavalry who were facing Sheridan.

March 31st. Sheridan was forced back a couple of miles. But his main object had been attained, for Lee, in order to save his flank, had been obliged to thin out his line at Petersburg.

April 1st, Five Forks. Sheridan, with all his cavalry and some infantry, attacked the Confederates who had taken up a position at Five Forks, and drove them northwards, taking 4,500 prisoners and six guns. But, when Sheridan followed them, a gap of six or eight miles of mud was left between him and the Federal main body, and he was exposed to a possible attack from the whole of Lee's army. To prevent Lee making such an attack Grant opened a heavy bombardment all along the lines, and gave orders for a general assault next day.

April 2nd. At 5 a.m. the assault was launched with success. The Confederates were driven out of their front line at nearly every point and pressed back to the inner defences of Petersburg.

April 3rd. Grant intended to complete his work by a final assault, but very early in the morning it was discovered that Lee had withdrawn his troops and was making the best of his way along the Danville Railway ; he ordered his four Corps who were spread out in the entrenchments to concentrate at Amelia Court House on the 4th. President Davis had been warned at midday on the 2nd that the city would be evacuated and that he must leave at once. At 8.15 a.m. on the 3rd the mayor of Richmond formally surrendered his city to General Weitzel, who marched in from the east.

As soon as Grant heard the news he turned all his troops westward to prevent Lee's escape. Sheridan might be relied on to do his part ; his one idea was to get ahead of Lee, if only with a handful of cavalry. But the infantry were not far behind ; there was no need to urge the men forward—without waiting for rations they pushed along, eager to be up at the finish which at last seemed to be within sight.

April 4th. Sheridan reached Jetersville while Lee was still at Amelia Court House, eight miles to the north-east.

April 5th. Two infantry Corps joined Sheridan. This forced Lee to turn aside from the direct road to Danville and make towards the Appomattox River.

April 6th. Two of Lee's Corps (Longstreet and Gordon) got away along the south bank of the Appomattox. But the other two Corps (Ewell and Anderson) were on a road farther south, making for Rice's Station, and were headed off by Sheridan. The Federal 6th Corps came up and a heavy engagement took place at Sailor's Creek. The whole of Ewell's Corps was forced to surrender, with its commander, also about half of Anderson's.

April 7th. Lee with his two remaining Corps crossed to the north bank of the Appomattox and took the road to Lynchburg. The bridges were set on fire to delay pursuit, but the Federals arrived in time to save one of them. This enabled the Federal 2nd Corps to cross to the north bank and hang on to Lee's tail, while Sheridan, on the south bank, was racing to get ahead of him. Lee halted, turned on his pursuers and drove their vanguard back. But the delay was fatal to the Southerners, for while they halted Sheridan was still on the move.

April 8th. Sheridan's cavalry reached Appomattox Station and captured some trains full of supplies which had been sent from Lynchburg to meet Lee. Then they took up a position for the night about three miles west of Appomattox Court House, on the road to Lynchburg. Lee was still to the east of them. There was no fighting during this day.

April 9th. Lee made one final effort to brush Sheridan out of his path ; as the Federals had only cavalry on the spot it seemed at first that the attempt might be successful. But Sheridan hung on and by 10 a.m. infantry began to come up to his support. The last hope of the South was gone, and Lee sent to ask for a meeting with Grant to arrange for surrender.

About 1 p.m. the two great antagonists met in the house of a Mr. McClean, near Appomattox Court House. Lee, tall, dignified, in full uniform ; Grant in a soldier's blouse with only shoulder straps to indicate his rank, desperately ill at ease ; he began talking of old days when they had been together in Mexico, and twice Lee had to remind him of the object of their meeting. The terms of surrender were generous : the whole army of the Confederates to be put on parole : officers to keep their swords : troopers and gunners to keep the horses which were their private property.

The strength of Lee's army was given as 28,356. On the 14th Johnston with 37,000 surrendered to Sherman near Goldsboro'. This ended the operations.

The end. There is no need to depict the relief of a nation at the sound of the ' Cease fire '—we have all felt that. But there was one more scene in the tragedy of America.

On the evening of April 14th the President with his wife and two friends went to Ford's Theatre in Washington. About ten o'clock a shot rang out, and Lincoln fell forward on the front of the box, unconscious and dying. The assassin was a half-mad actor, John W. Booth ; he was leader of a conspiracy which plotted to murder several members of the Government, but the others were unharmed except Seward, who was wounded in his own house. Three of the band were afterwards arrested and hanged. Booth himself sprang from the box to the stage, injuring his leg as he fell ; he managed to get away on a horse that was waiting at the stage door. Some days later he was shot in a barn which had been set on fire by the soldiers who were pursuing him.

Lincoln was carried to a house near the theatre, where he died early next morning without recovering consciousness. Stanton, who watched over him, said— ' Now he belongs to the ages.'

XXI

CONCLUSION

A MAN may be a great statesman and yet a hopeless muddler in the science of war. Such was the younger Pitt ; he was the soul of European coalitions, his courage and intellectual powers have never been questioned ; but during his administration the land forces of England were frittered away in expeditions which were badly planned, badly commanded, and badly carried out.[1] The blame may be laid on his military advisers, but had he been a strategist he would have recognized their weakness.

To set a true value on Lincoln as a strategist we must shut our eyes to the glamour which surrounds the statesman and get down to his military work. Pictures have been drawn which put him in rather a pathetic light, struggling to fathom a subject too deep for his powers : bombarded with advice, good and bad, interested and disinterested, from soldiers and politicians, from semi-independent Governors of States, from very independent journalists : firm in the determination to gain his end but acting only as a hindrance to his army :[2] yes, of course he was a great man, but he knew nothing of war—how could he ? —and of course he did his best, but the inference is that it could not have been much worse.

Well—to get at some standard by which Lincoln can be measured let us look for a moment at ourselves in

[1] Expeditions in 1793 to Toulon and Belgium, in 1795 to Quiberon, in 1798 to Lisbon, in 1805 to Naples.

[2] Henderson, vol. i, p. 407 ; ' The mistakes of Lincoln and Stanton are not to be condoned by pointing to McClellan.'

Vol. ii, p. 5 : ' In assuming control of the Union armies Lincoln and Stanton made their enemies a present of at least 50,000 men.'

1914. A big nation suddenly plunged into a war for which the standing army was quite inadequate. At the head of affairs a somewhat mysterious Authority, which we now call the Higher Command, formed from the Cabinet and expert advisers. It was the Higher Command which made or approved plans for co-operation with our Allies ; dealt with the question of man-power and the expansion of the army ; arranged co-ordination of the naval, military, and air forces, and decided on the distribution of them. Certain troops were reserved for home defence and for the garrison of strategic points like the Suez Canal. It was certain that France would be the theatre of decisive operations, so the main body was sent there—but the commander of the main body had no powers over forces outside France. Though it may be a matter of argument whether the distribution was wisely made, there is no doubt that in a war of nations the Higher Command is a necessary part of war organization. It deals with all the broad plans in which consideration must be given to such factors as politics, finance, industry ; only after these are settled can we get down to pure strategy and tactics in the field.

There is no shame in admitting that in 1914 our ideas on strategy and tactics had to be very much revised. To take simple examples. Much time used to be spent in teaching infantry ' control of rifle fire '—and out of the millions of rounds fired in the war not one was ever controlled. Text-books on strategy were full of flank attacks—' a blow on the flank or rear is more decisive than a blow on the front '—but when the enemy stretched from the sea to the Alps there was no flank to aim at ; two sides faced each other for four years with barely a hundred yards between their front lines. Improvements in firearms, the invention of new weapons, the march of science, all produced conditions to which past experience was no guide. We must admit the fact that the battle-field of the future is like an uncharted sea.

Such remarks may seem to be hinting that the study of strategy and tactics is useless. I certainly mean nothing of the sort. A seaman sails into an uncharted sea, but knowledge and experience teach him to avoid rocks and shoals where a land-lubber would come to grief. In the same way a professional soldier will pick up his bearings on an uncharted battle-field and set a true course, where an amateur will be lost.

My case is that Lincoln kept a true course by strength of character and the light of sheer genius.

It is not claimed that he made no mistakes. ' The history of war is the history of mistakes '—so says Napoleon, and he ought to know, for he made plenty of them. His brilliant victories are put in the scale against the mistakes, and on the balance he is acclaimed as a great strategist. In the foregoing chapters I have dealt with definite charges which have been brought against Lincoln—and on the whole he has a wonderfully clean record.

But a verdict of ' Not guilty ' is very negative praise —we must look for positive virtues, and perhaps his attitude on command of the sea comes first.

Command of the Sea. To us, with experience of centuries as a Naval Power, the value of command of the sea is obvious, so much so that we are apt to forget that it is not always obvious to other people. At the outset of the Civil War it does not seem to have been realized by the Americans, though later on they understood it thoroughly. The belief was that the rebellion would soon collapse. Various measures were being urged on the President by Congress, by the press, by private advisers, but I have failed to find a record of anything which urged the importance of the blockade. Records show that the fleet was raised from forty-two ships in

1861 to 671 in 1864; a large amount of organization, and money, and labour must have been expended to work up such an increase; it could not have been undertaken without direct authority from the President, and he would not have given that authority unless he had been firmly convinced in his forecast of the course of the war.

The object was to prevent the export of cotton or the import of warlike stores and other articles which the South could not produce for itself. Slowly but surely the blockade spread its tentacles along 3,000 miles of coast and down the Mississippi, till the Confederacy was held in its grip, isolated from the commerce of the world. As a factor in the war it was of inestimable value.

In addition to this duty the U.S. Navy had a separate one—protection of its own commerce. The Confederates had few warships, and they saw the impossibility of blockading the enemy's ports, so they could only cripple the commerce of the North by preying on merchant vessels on the high seas. In this they were very active, chiefly by means of ships purchased in England.

The most famous of the commerce destroyers was the *Alabama*. She was launched from the yard of Laird & Sons at Birkenhead, near Liverpool. In July 1862 she slipped out to sea on the pretext of making a trial of engines—and disappeared. In the Azores she was handed over to a Confederate commander, Capt. Semmes, and started on her career. During the next two years she roamed the Atlantic and even made trips into Indian and Chinese waters; she captured about sixty vessels in all. In June 1864 the American Consul at Cherbourg reported her arrival in that port. The U.S.S. *Kearsage* hung off the coast until she came outside, and in a great duel which followed the *Alabama* was sunk.

There were other ships, such as the *Florida* and *Georgia*, on similar errands. On the whole the damage they did was not great, but it might have grown to serious dimensions had not Lincoln cut it off at the root. It is scarcely too much to say that the battle for protection of commerce was fought out in the British Foreign Office.

In 1863 there were three ships in the yard of Laird & Sons. Ostensibly they were built to the order of a French purchaser, but there was little doubt at the time, and there is no doubt now, that the French sheepskin was a thin disguise for the Confederate wolf. The ships were powerful ironclads : they would be a serious menace to commerce : they might be strong enough to raise the blockade : they might even threaten the ports of the North. The American Minister in London, C. F. Adams, sent in very strong representations to the British Foreign Minister, Lord John Russell, asking that the vessels might be detained : in one letter (dated September 5th), after referring to the refusal of the Government to take action, he said—' It would be superfluous in me to point out to your lordship that this is war.'

These words were not bluff. Adams wrote in his diary, ' I clearly foresee that collision must now come of it '—and no doubt he had communicated this conviction to Washington.

Russell had been in a pretty diplomatic mess ever since the *Alabama* left England. His perplexities were serious at the time, but it is hard to repress a smile when we look back on them. Wise men had been telling the Government that the South would certainly win independence ; the Southerners were all for free trade, and bought largely in the British market ; and though they were slave-owners, which is very wrong, a prudent shopkeeper does not inquire too closely into the morals of a good customer. England had declared neutrality : legal opinion on International Law said that ' you may sell muskets to one party or the other . . . but if you allow a ship to be armed and go at once to make an attack on a foreign belligerent, you are taking part in the war : ' the opinion of shipbuilders was that such a view was neither neutral nor fair, and, as the Federals had been allowed to buy the munitions they wanted, the Confederates should be allowed to buy the ships they wanted : other people had opinions which counted for little, but votes which counted for much.

A very pretty diplomatic mess. It was Adams who cleared it up and simplified the problem ; he eliminated the legal and commercial factors by reducing it to the plain proposition—the ships must be detained or ' this is war '. Lincoln had already made emancipation the main issue : whatever might be the interests of individuals or the opinion of the Law, the British Nation could not and would not join in the war on the side that upheld slavery. When the problem was stated in the simple terms of Adams the Government could not hesitate about the solution. The ships were detained, and, after the mysterious French purchaser had been forgotten, were bought for the British Navy. And this was peace.

The firm diplomacy of Adams was beyond all praise, but the real strength of his arguments lay in the instructions he received from Washington. It was Lincoln who faced the prospect of war sooner than submit to interference with the blockade. This gives us a clear measure of the value he put on Command of the Sea.

Land Forces. When dealing with the distribution of forces, ' the strategical deployment ', it must be kept in mind that when a democratic country goes to war the Government has to rely on the people, not only for soldiers, but for money and supplies of every kind—

also for moral support and votes : in return for this support the people expect protection for their homes and industries. The result is that the defensive policy calls for more attention than in the days of war between rival autocrats, who were not obliged to consider the personal interests of their subjects.

Political interests of this kind had much weight in deciding the distribution of the Federal forces. Lincoln felt that he could not afford to allow the enemy to occupy border States, and the result was a wide deployment which at first sight seems contrary to sound strategy. But if we look deeper I think it was advisable even from a purely military point of view. The theory of the ' offensive mass ' is thoroughly Napoleonic, and no doubt it sounds easy to say that 300,000 men could have been collected, as suggested by McClellan in his first scheme. The practical difficulties, however, are serious, especially with a raw army in a country like Virginia. The staff was untrained ; there were few roads, fewer railways ; an army of such size could not subsist on the country ; it would be tied to its line of supply, and this means loss of mobility. In '64 Grant had just over 120,000 in the Wilderness ; his Quartermaster's Department had learnt the handling of transport, and the difficulties of supply were successfully overcome. But if the force had been doubled I think it would have come to a halt through the dead weight of its own numbers. Compare Napoleon's mass in Russia in 1812. By separating into smaller armies the questions of supply and transport were simplified and consequently mobility was increased.

But, with a wide deployment, it is necessary to keep in view the great maxim which was afterwards the guiding principle of Von Moltke—every one of the separate units must pull its weight. Lincoln seems to have grasped this all-important point. During '62 and '63 he was constantly urging Buell and Rosecrans to

' do something '. The orders were vague, and give rise to the idea that he was impatient, unreasonable, incapable of understanding military movements. The generals raised objections which may have been sound from the local point of view—but they could not see beyond their own horizon. The duty of the Higher Command is to survey the whole theatre of war. A unit which is ' doing something ', even doing it badly, may be giving great help to somebody else. In the same way that Lincoln urged Hooker to ' put in all his men ', so he himself was trying to put in all his separate armies.

As regards Washington, it was unfortunately in an exposed position, on the very frontier, but its political importance was so great that all the military advisers agreed in the necessity for defending it. McClellan, though he agreed in principle, differed as to the best means of carrying it out ; he clung to the maxim that attack is always the best defence, and applied this by saying that ' the defence of Washington lies on the banks of the James River '. My opinion on this point has been given in Chapter IX—to the effect that whatever may have been the correct solution as judged by mere numbers, Lincoln was right in putting the human factor into the scale. And to this may now be added an example from the Great War : while the British were concentrating an offensive mass for the battle of the Somme in 1916, they were careful to leave a strong line to cover Calais—in other words, they did not think that the defence of Calais lay on the banks of the Somme.

We see that Lincoln was carrying out all the functions of the modern Higher Command. There was no ready-made General Staff to set carefully prepared plans before him, and he had to pick up expert advice as best he could. There is no doubt that he felt the necessity for expert advice and was earnestly in search of a competent adviser. The rapid succession of McClellan, Pope, Halleck, Burnside, and Hooker gives weight to the suggestion that he was unreasonably impatient. To this there are several replies. First, a satisfactory Commander-in-Chief is not easily found, as may be seen from the fact that in the Great War there were changes in the command of nearly all the armies : second, not one of the generals mentioned was really fit for the post: third, if Lincoln could not make a good commander he could at least recognize one when he saw him—and he was the first to recognize Grant.

After Grant had taken control nothing more is heard about impatience or interference, and many writers are high in praise of Lincoln's attitude : he had ' muddled through ' the early stages in accordance with Anglo-Saxon tradition, but was quite intelligent and could learn : so he ended up as a sensible statesman, leaving military affairs to those who understood them. Lord Wolseley says :

' In the first three years of the Secession War, when Mr. Lincoln and Mr. Stanton practically controlled the movements of the Federal forces, the Confederates were generally sucessful. . . . The Northern prospects did not begin to brighten until Mr. Lincoln, in March '64, with that unselfish intelligence which distinguished him, abdicated his military functions in favour of General Grant.'

With these words I disagree most emphatically. To begin with, there is a mistake in facts ; the Northern prospects began to brighten with Gettysburg and Vicksburg, long before Lincoln ' abdicated ' ; the first five months of Grant's reign were anything but bright.

Grant was a really great soldier—the campaign of Vicksburg was a masterpiece : he made some mistakes, as did Frederick the Great, Napoleon, and all the other commanders in history : his worst mistake was when he left the road to Washington open to Early. The fall of the Capital would have been taken as a convincing proof of the Democrats' assertion that ' the war is a failure ' ; the brain staggers in trying to think out what the further results might have been if the Democrats had won the election of '64. In a war of Nations the soldier needs the help of the statesman. If they shut themselves up in watertight compartments the natural result is the situation of July '64—Grant with 120,000 men hammering at the gates of one Capital, Early with 17,000 walking up unopposed to the gates of the other.

War is in itself a crime against humanity and civilization, but if we find ourselves involved in the crime there is no need to make a blunder of it. Surely the time has come to recognize that civilian help does not of necessity imply civilian interference. The whole idea of the Higher Command is to harness together the best brains in the country for the purposes of war, just as a Cabinet forms a team for purposes of peace ; each member has his own job, but success depends on the team pulling together under the control of one man. Lincoln was the right man to handle a team ; he could dominate without domineering, he could help when help was wanted. But, in a generous desire to put Grant at his ease, he effaced himself too much, and in withdrawing his control he also withdrew his assistance. My admiration for Lincoln is enthusiastic, but I look on the ' abdication ' as the least wise of all his acts.

Let us look back at what he did before Grant came on the scene : the blockade, emancipation, conscription. Look at his letters to McClellan [1] and Hooker [2] and the letter he wrote but did not send to Meade.[3]

Could Grant or any other strategist have written with clearer foresight or deeper understanding ? The difficulties are not shirked ; he faces squarely and frankly the weak point of his own army, want of discipline in the higher ranks ; there is no hint of inter-

[1] *Ante*, p. 111.   [2] *Ante*, pp. 153, 161, 162.   [3] *Ante*, p. 170.

ference with the tactics of the battle-field, but the main objective is written large—' I think that Lee's army and not Richmond is your main objective '—' In the next battle put in all your men.'

Compare Napoleon's words—' There are many generals in Europe, but as a rule they see too many things ; as for me I see only one thing, the main body of the enemy.' Lincoln saw the one thing from the first.

The interesting light that is thrown backwards by the Great War shows that Lincoln had a fine perception of the duties of the Higher Command.

1. From the first moment he realized the value of superior naval power and made the most of it.

2. The strategic deployment fitted in with political considerations and at the same time was well suited to the conditions of a raw army.

3. The principle of maintaining pressure all along the line was constantly urged.

4. The chief objective, the main body of the enemy, was kept in view with a true sense of perspective.

5. There were no half measures. The questions of the Union and Emancipation were to be settled in such a way that they could never be reopened. This could only be done by destroying completely the military forces of the enemy

These broad principles were faultless—it was in the execution of them that faults must be admitted. Some of these were due to the commanders in the field, some to Lee's weight on the other side, a good many to the absence of any ready-made machinery for the administration of large forces. There is, however, a balance which must be put down to Lincoln's account. To take an instance—the garrison of Washington in April 1861. The broad principle, laid down by a council of senior officers and approved by the President, was that the minimum should be 35,000 men : administrative steps ought to have been taken at once to appoint a commandant and give him an opportunity to satisfy himself that the troops were adequate in numbers and efficiency. The omission to do so was a bad mistake and spoilt any chances which the Peninsular scheme might have had.

Such cases show that the Higher Command must have a strong element of professional knowledge and experience, and I am far from suggesting that Lincoln was in himself an ideal High Command. His genius comes out in the fact that he was aware of his own deficiencies and sought to remedy them, while, in the matters in which he felt himself competent, he had absolute confidence in his own judgement. It was not the confidence of a Napoleon, who could only see one side of an argument, the side that fitted in with his own wishes. Lincoln could see various sides, and would even appear to be arguing against himself—so much so that it left an impression of hesitation and doubt. But though he did not jump to conclusions, he could make up his mind with a confidence that showed clear judgement and iron determination.

Is there anything pathetic in this picture ? There was tragedy in the human side of it—a man who hated war sending forth his countrymen to death. But pathetic is not the right word for the Commander-in-Chief : some moments of disappointment, anxiety, impatience, such as must come to every commander when big issues are at stake, no moments of weakness. The position of Dictator was thrust upon him by circumstances; he accepted it, not from personal ambition but because he felt himself to be a bigger man than those around him ; having accepted it, he made full use of his power. We see a very masterful Dictator issuing the first call to arms, instituting the blockade, proclaiming emancipation, warding off the intervention of foreign Powers—to say nothing of ruling a nation of free-born Anglo-Saxons.

The Anglo-Saxons grumbled at him and disagreed with him, as is their free-born manner, and voted for him and supported him, as is also their manner ; and so fought their way to victory.

'In war the men are nothing ; it is the man who is everything.' That is an exaggeration—there were many men who earned immortal fame and helped to hold the Union together. But the man was Abraham Lincoln.

INDEX

Names of Confederate officers are printed in italics.

'Merrimac', Confederate ship, 70, 71, 94, 96.
Miles, Gen., 47.
Mill Springs, battle of, 178.
Milroy, Gen., 85, 86, 161.
'Monitor', U. S. S. 70, 71.
Morgan, Col., 181.
Morton, Governor, 183.
Mosby, Col., 222.
Murfreesboro, battle of, 184.

Nashville, battle of, 219.

Owens, Miss M., 25.

Patterson, Gen., 47, 50, 51.
Paxson, Professor, 16, 45, 63.
Pemberton, Gen., 191, 192.
Perryville, battle of, 182, 183.
Pettigrew, Gen., 167.
Pickett, Gen., 167.
Pittsburg Landing, battle of, See Shiloh.
Pope, Gen., ch. x, 121, 146, 169, 181, 237.
Porter, Admiral, 191.
Porter, Gen., 98, 99, 120, 127.
Port Hudson, surrender of, 192.
Port Republic, battle of, 88.

Raymond, battle of, 191.
Reynolds, Gen., 165.
Rhodes, J. F., 144, 167, 170, 184.
Ropes, J. C., 35, 72, 103, 110, 117, 136, 146, 178.
Rosecrans, Gen., 183, 184, 194–7, 235.
Runyon, Gen., 47.
Russell, Lord John, 63, 140, 233, 234.
Rutledge, Miss A., 24.

'San Jacinta', U. S. S., 64.
Sailor's Creek, battle of, 227.
Savage Station, battle of, 100.

Schofield, Gen., 216, 219.
Scott, Gen. Winfield, 31, 32, 35, 49, 54, 58, 67, 68, 103, 104, 175.
Sedgwick, Gen., 154, 155, 158, 159, 205.
Semmes, Capt., 232.
Seven Days, battles, ch. viii.
Seven Pines, battle of, See Fair Oaks.
Seward, Secretary, 28, 29, 30, 140, 228.
Seymour, Governor, 220.
Sharpsburg, battle of, See Antietam.
Sheridan, Gen., 113, 205, 206, 212–15, 221, 224–7.
Sherman, Gen., 113, 190, 198, 199, 204, 215–19, 221–4, 228.
Shields, Gen., 83, 84, 85, 87, 88.
Shiloh, battle of, 180, 181.
Sigel, Gen., 116, 204, 210.
Slidell, J., 64.
Smith, Gen. C. F., 185.
Smith, Gen. Kirby, 51, 53, 56, 57, 182, 183.
Smith, Gen. W. F., 94, 131, 132, 207.
Spotsylvania Court House, battle of, 206, 207.
Stanton, Secretary, 30, 31, 121, 131–3, 187, 197, 203, 204, 228, 229, 237.
Stoneman, Gen., 154.
Stone's River, battle of, See Murfreesboro.
Stuart, Gen. J. E. B., 51, 100, 101, 117, 118, 155, 162, 163, 206.
Sumner, Gen., 71, 97, 121, 126, 127, 146, 148, 149, 150.
Sumter, Fort, 35, 36.

Thomas, Gen. (Adjt. Gen.), 75.
Thomas, Gen. G. H., 196–9, 216, 218, 219.
Todd, Miss M., 25.

PUBLISHER'S NOTE: This new edition of *The Military Genius of Abraham Lincoln* by the late Brigadier-General Colin R. Ballard is a facsimile reprint of the original book, which in less than a quarter-century has become a recognized classic of American military and political history, and a collector's item as well.

Although there are a few minor factual errors in the work, we have not felt at liberty to alter the author's original text. However, attention should be called to the fact that the letters quoted on pages 111, 153 and 170 contain minor inaccuracies both in wording and in punctuation, which however do not affect the sense. This edition is the one approved by the author at the time of its original publication.